Today's families come in all shapes and sizes, but the passion for family and the need to nurture and support them is universal. In fact, finding practical ways to meet the competing demands in our lives is one of the greatest challenges businesses face today. Congratulations on your latest tool to help families find solutions that work!

Dick Kearns, Vice Chairman, Price Waterhouse LLP
Chairman, Smart Families/Smart Business

Send me twenty-four copies today! I want my friends with young families to get started on this 30 Days to a Smart Family ... ASAP!

Bobb Biehl
President, Masterplanning Group International

This is a book that will call families everywhere to action. 30 Days to a Smart Family, obligates us to look deep inside ourselves and identify what matters most—right here in our own homes.

Hyrum W. Smith, Chairman of the Board
and Chief Executive Officer, Franklin-Covey Company

This book could revolutionize military families. A hopeful, positive, dynamic book. It is the antidote for societal resources to put family second.

G. D. Gibson
Commander, CHC, U.S. Navy; Head, Plans Branch,
Office of the Chief of Chaplains

In the hectic world in which we live, Paul Lewis and Thom Black have created an important parable for each of us to read and to contemplate—made all the more powerful by the fact that it is based on a true story. No father—or mother—will be able to read this book without engaging in serious self-examination. Each will be better for having done so. And so will those around them.

Dr. Wade Horn
President, The National Fatherhood Initiative

In 30 Days to a Smart Family authors Lewis and Black map out a gold mine of helpful tips and suggestions guaranteed to raise your family's I.Q.—in just 30 days!

David and Claudia Arp
Founders, Marriage Alive International

You won't have to mine very long to find the gold in 30 Days to a Smart Family. Paul Lewis and Thom Black inspired me to appreciate my family more, and that's something I can start doing today!

Mike Yorkey
Editor-in-Chief, Focus on the Family magazines

Because Americans are impatient, thrive on choice, and love a challenge, 30 Days to a Smart Family provides a great way for us to put our best intentions to work and get the most out of life.

Josh Hammond
Author, The Stuff Americans Are Made Of:
The Seven Cultural Forces That Define Americans

This simple and profound message shot into my heart. The story and the principles continue to inspire and challenge me long after reading this book.

Jim Burns
President, National Institute of Youth Ministry

While reading this book on an airplane, the woman next to me saw the title and showed interest. I loaned it to her for the next thirty minutes. Upon completion, she asked how she could obtain a copy. It had already made an impact on her! This book should be read with the idea that you will share it with someone else when you finish. And the real fun begins when you get to the second half of the book and can began to apply it in your own life.

Mary Ellen Pollock,
Lifestyle Education Manager, Wellness Services
Winter Park Health Foundation, Florida

Our society will live or die on the strength of our families. My favorite line in this book is "There is nothing so precious as your family." 30 Days helps to put our sporadic thoughts and desires about improving our family into a clear productive plan.

Stan Smith,
Professional tennis player

What an amazing and wonderful journey! This book is an experience no family should miss. Thanks Paul and Thom, for helping us "think smart."

Drs. Les and Leslie Parrott
Founders, Center for Relationship Development,
Seattle Pacific University

As I was reading 30 Days to a Smart Family, I mentally made a list of all the people in my life I needed to share my appreciation with. I started thinking—what if they only had 30 days to live? What would I want them to know about how I feel about them. This kind of thinking sure makes the world a kinder, more nurturing place. Imagine what could be accomplished in that kind of environment!

Holly Parks, Managing Partner,
Human Resource Institute, St. Charles, Illinois

Of the many rich rewards a family will gain, one quite unique to 30 Days is the way it engages those who are not team members or naturally disposed to group activities. Finally, a means for including all the budding artists, scientists, scholars, engineers, writers, and deep sea divers in the family circle.

Art Miller
Founder, President, People Management Inc.

We need a newer, richer vision of what the family can be today. Paul and Thom have given us that vision and a usable vehicle to get there. This is a great book. I urge you to read it and put it to work!

Dr. Ron Jensen
Chairman, Future Achievement International

Paul Lewis and Thom Black have done it again! In this quick read they have identified concisely where my treasures lie and how to mine them. They will you too. A must read.

Tim Templeton
President, Providence Seminars, Inc.

This book changes the way you see your family forever. Anyone looking to improve communication and relationships and to build their family life will truly benefit from this insightful book.

Marie Knight, Community Services Manager
City of Garden Grove, California

Lewis and Black pulled me into the book with a powerful story that can't be ignored. Then the book becomes creatively interactive in very practical ways. As a CEO, it made me think much more about my responsibility to nurture family health in our organization. And that includes my own family. This is a timely wake-up call, but one with relevant solutions.

Dr. Robert C. Andringa
President, Coalition for Christian Colleges & Universities

Paul and Thom have used this powerful allegory to reach deep below the surface and touch the heart of our need. We can't help but be challenged as we see our own situations in this story. Then, they give us the tools for practical life application so we can do what we need to do—now!

Barry Durman
President, Atlantic City Rescue Mission

30 DAYS to a SMART FAMILY

Paul Lewis and Thom Black

FAMILY UNIVERSITY

ZondervanPublishingHouse
Grand Rapids, Michigan

A Division of HarperCollinsPublishers

30 Days to a Smart Family
Copyright © 1997 by Family University, LLC

Requests for information should be addressed to:

≝ ZondervanPublishingHouse
Grand Rapids, Michigan 49530

Library of Congress Cataloging-in-Publication Data

Lewis, Paul, 1994.
   30 days to a smart family : the family life you dream of just became possible /
Paul Lewis and Thom Black.
      p.   cm.
      ISBN: 0-310-21585-4 (Hardcover)
    1. Family counseling. 2. Family. I. Black, Thom. II. Title.
HQ10.L46   1997
646.7'8—dc21   96-47821
                                             CIP

This edition printed on acid-free paper and meets the American National
Standards Institute Z39.48 standard.

Interior illustrations by Chris Sharp
Interior design by Paul Lewis

Printed in the United States of America

---

97 98 99 00 01 02 03 04 /❖ DC/ 10 9 8 7 6 5 4 3 2 1

*To all who will
discover with us that
each present moment
contains the
family treasure
of life itself.*

Contents

Part I

❧

The Story

Prologue

STOP!

This is a warning. If you are a thoughtful person, the story you are about to read could change you forever.

How?

Close your eyes for a moment and ponder afresh the meaning of a very familiar word:

family.

Can you think of that word without a flood of feelings and memories—the good and the bad—hopes and fears, joys and pains filling your mind?

Many of life's defining moments are crafted and shared with family.

What would your life be like if all of that were suddenly . . . gone?

Turn that question over in your mind.

Again.

Now, turn the page.

Once there was a man who had devoted his life to helping families.

Day in, day out, for years and years he had listened to families, counseled families, worried about families.

But lately he had begun to wonder if he was making much of a difference in the lives of the people who came to him for help.

On this particular day, he sat behind his desk, impatiently tapping his pencil against his knee as he stared blankly at the couple bickering in front of him. The minutes were dragging by.

With each new hour, each new session, each new family, his feeling of fruitlessness had grown. His struggle over what to do about it worried him so, his work had almost become too much to bear. He saw so many people with so many problems. And even as he offered his knowledge and help, he'd begun to notice how little improvement he ever saw in his clients.

If we know so much about how to have successful families, he kept asking himself, why can't I make families stronger? He found himself growing ever more cynical, even to the point of wondering if there was any such thing as a strong family.

He had never felt more powerless.

That night he came home from work exhausted and unspeakably dejected. He did not even have the energy to talk with his kids or his wife. He certainly could not bring himself to confide in her his secret doubts about his inability to change things for the better. And so, even in his own home, with all the knowledge he'd acquired, relationships were less than healthy.

His wife had noticed all of this. She was concerned about how his lack of energy had begun to affect their family. But she knew her husband's heart and was waiting for this weariness to pass, for his energy and focus to return.

What she did not know was the depths of his despondency over his powerlessness to effect real change in his world. But something had happened to her that day, and she was eager to tell him all about it. She sat down on the couch, where he had plopped for the night.

"The strangest thing happened on the way to work this morning," she began. "I was standing by myself, waiting for my train, when a man came up, introduced himself, and started asking questions about you."

Her husband turned and asked cautiously, "Why would he ask you questions about me?"

"I don't know," she answered. "But he knew what you did for a living, and he asked if you seemed happy with your work. He wanted to know if you felt like you were really helping people."

This bothered the man considerably. "You didn't tell him anything, did you?"

"Not at first," his wife said. "But he seemed genuine. Nice. He said many of his employees had come to you for help, so I felt it was all right."

The man frowned. "You shouldn't have told a complete stranger anything—you know that."

But his wife was unconcerned. "I had this sense about him. He wasn't a troublemaker. I could tell he had something weighty on his mind. It seemed . . . important." She got up then and walked across the room to retrieve her satchel. "He gave me his phone number and asked me to give it to you." She pulled a scrap of paper from her satchel and held it out to her husband. "Here."

The man could only stare at the paper in disbelief. "I'm not calling anyone. I have my hands full now with people coming to my office with their problems. I don't need to be adding phone clients as well."

The woman sighed. "Suit yourself," she said, placing the piece of paper in her husband's lap. "But he was not a kook, and the last thing he said was that he had a story to tell you, one he thought you'd thank him for."

Then she went to bed.

The man eyed the scrap of paper. Everyone has a story, he thought. He listened to people's stories all day long. He was certain he had heard every story in the world. What would make this one different from the others? And why would he ever thank someone for having to listen to another one?

The man sat on the couch without moving for several minutes, staring down at the scrap in his lap. He had no energy for mysterious strangers or for any new stories. Just going to work took all the energy he had.

So the man crumpled the paper and threw it at the trash basket by his briefcase. And, wearily, he went to bed, too.

Sleep didn't come easily for the man. He couldn't get the fellow on the train platform out of his mind. What did the stranger truly know about him? And why didn't he just set up an appointment like other clients? And how could any story be so important that he would approach the man's wife, dangling the promise that he would thank the stranger for hearing it? For all his weariness, the man could not help but wonder about something so unusual.

Finally, somewhere after midnight, the man slid out of bed and plodded into the living room. He flicked on a light and rummaged in the little trash basket for the scrap.

It wasn't there.

He looked all around the basket, but no phone number. The paper seemed to have vanished.

"Oh well, one more thread woven into the mysterious tapestry of life," he mused poetically as he yawned, turned out the light, and slowly stumbled back to the bedroom.

Still, he wondered, now more than ever, what it was all about. He pulled the covers up around him, snuggled his body up against his sleeping wife, and reflected on the strange intruder.

❦   ❦   ❦

The next morning the man walked into the living room to retrieve his briefcase and noticed something underneath it.

The scrap of paper.

"How did it get there?" he murmured, certain he had looked there last night.

The man bent down and picked it up, then unfolded it for the first time. Sure enough, inside the note was a phone number.

And there was more—in bold handwriting—a name: "Mark Fairchild."

The man still felt uneasy, however, unable to imagine what had prompted Fairchild's unusual actions. Why would someone give his name and number to a woman he did not know? What story could be important enough for a person to take such extraordinary steps to seek out a stranger in such an unusual way?

He stuffed the paper into his pants pocket. Story or no, the man told himself, I will have to think about this.

🍎   🍎   🍎

"Mark Fairchild, please."

"This is Fairchild."

Silence.

The man, holding the phone to his ear, had no idea why he had stopped in the middle of his day, taken out the scrap of paper, and dialed the number.

And now here was this Fairchild on the other end of the phone line. The man knew that if he went one word further he wouldn't be able to turn back.

He did not have time for this. He should hang up.

Now.

But the man's weariness had yet to totally vanquish his sense of possibility. So he spoke the next word.

"Yes ... Mr. Fairchild. You talked with my wife yesterday on the train platform, gave her a note, and asked me to call. She said you had some sort of unusual story for me? How can I help you?"

Fairchild was silent.

The man cradled the phone against his ear for what seemed a full minute, waiting for a response from this Fairchild fellow.

"Mr. Fairchild?"

Finally, in a voice surprisingly collected and firm after such a pause, Mr. Fairchild spoke. "I wondered if you'd call. And I'm grateful that you did. Your wife was very cordial yesterday. I apologize for what I'm sure to you seems to be, at best, odd behavior on my part. I was a bit insistent with her, but she was most gracious."

"Well," said the man, switching the phone to his other ear, "I'm sure you can appreciate my hesitating even to make this call. It would not be uncommon in my line of work to be dealing with a disgruntled family member of one of my clients, or worse. I can't be too careful."

Mr. Fairchild sighed as if he bore a great weight on his shoulders. "Yes, I can imagine the tensions of your job, working with families today. There is so much to lose, isn't there? So much of what is done goes by so quickly and yet lasts so—very—forever in the lives of all concerned. Doesn't it?"

"Well, yes . . ." The man hesitated, wondering at such words and, from long experience, the meaning between the lines. "Well, no harm done." He began to impatiently tap his pencil on his desk. "What exactly was it you wanted?" He reached for his appointment book. "Would you like to schedule an appointment to talk with me?"

Fairchild laughed softly. "No, sir, I believe you should schedule an appointment to see me."

That stopped the man. He did not know what to think.

"I believe," Fairchild went on, "considering the line of work you are in, you should consider the story I have to tell you. And consider it well."

The man nervously ran his hand through his hair, slightly irritated now, the weariness drifting near again. He never should have picked up the phone number. This was getting more complicated by the moment.

"Make an appointment to see you? Mr. Fairchild, why don't you just tell me the story over the phone? That will save everybody time, and we can get back to the business of our day."

He could feel Fairchild's displeasure come rushing over the phone line.

"Maybe you shouldn't worry so much about your busyness and be more concerned with what is important," Fairchild said in a surprisingly serious tone. "I'm telling you that I have a story for you that you must hear, that I need to tell you. What could be more important?"

The man felt sheepish, embarrassed that a person he didn't even know could so effectively deliver a deserved rebuke. Hadn't he spoken the same words to clients for years?

"All right," he told Fairchild. "I will take you up on that challenge. When and where do we meet?"

"The park at the corner of School Street and Grant," Fairchild said quickly, as if he knew the man's response before it was spoken. "There is a green bench to the right of the fountain. I'll meet you there at noon."

"Noon today?" The man glanced at the grandfather clock in his office. It was already ten-thirty. "Does it have to be today?"

Again the voice was firm and uncompromising. "I'm sorry, but yes. I have begun scheduling important things for my 'todays.' This is one of them."

The resolve in Fairchild's voice moved the man to relent. "All right. See you at noon."

The man hung up, checked his watch, stared at the pile of work on his desk, shook his head—and sighed. What was he getting himself into?

❦ ❦ ❦

"Mr. Fairchild?"

The man looked down at the figure sitting on the bench. Fairchild looked to be in his fifties. He was well-groomed, appearing comfortable in his three-piece suit. He had a rather composed, in-control presence about him.

The man relaxed. His wife was right. This fellow didn't appear to be a kook.

"Mind if I sit down?" he asked Fairchild.

Fairchild stared up at the man, and the man recognized the sadness clouding his eyes. He had seen it many times in the faces of his clients.

"No," answered Fairchild. "Please sit down."

As he scooted over to make room on the bench, Fairchild turned sideways to face the man, his eyes burrowing into the man's own, as if he were searching for something.

It made the man very uncomfortable.

"I have heard good things about you," Fairchild said. "I've heard you care a great deal about what goes on in people's homes. I heard you give of yourself to your clients, helping families rebuild themselves. You've helped many people I know."

The man shrugged wearily at this unexpected flattery, especially since he felt quite the opposite about himself. This wasn't what he expected to hear.

The man leaned back a bit from Fairchild to get a larger look at what was unfolding. "Exactly what is this all about, Mr. Fairchild?"

Fairchild looked past the man, off into the distance.

"Twelve months ago, my best friend, a man about your age, died of liver cancer. He was a soulmate to me. I loved him very much." Fairchild's voice betrayed deep feelings. He blinked several times as if holding back overdue grief.

Instinctively, out of long, caring habit, the man touched Fairchild's shoulder for a moment with a sympathetic hand. "I'm so sorry."

Fairchild's head dropped a bit as he continued. "He had seemed healthy enough, in his mid-forties. Wonderful family. Wonderful wife. There was no clue that anything was wrong. He went to the doctor for some routine blood work and was told he had thirty days to live. Just like that ..." Fairchild shook his head slowly.

The man shifted a bit uncomfortably on the hard bench. This was no place to be counseling a grief victim.

"Mr. Fairchild, why don't you make an appointment to stop by my office and—"

•

"No, friend." Fairchild straightened up, his eyes again alive and his voice reclaiming the firmness he had exhibited over the phone. "I told you I had a story for you and indeed I do. I want you to see and hear what happened to this man's family during his last days. It was the most amazing thing I have ever seen."

The man was becoming slightly curious. "All right," he said.

"I have been around families my whole life," Fairchild went on. "Have a family of my own. But never have I seen what I witnessed in that home during my friend's last days and in the days since his death."

The man was now definitely curious. "What happened?"

"One of those things you see more than hear and sense more than can be told. An amazing transformation." Fairchild coughed, apologized, coughed again.

Then he stood up, surprising the man. After all, the man thought he was about to hear a story. Instead, Fairchild handed the man a piece of scrap paper, just like the one he'd given the man's wife.

"I could tell you the story," Fairchild said. "But it's not really my story to tell. You need to talk with my friend's wife. Please. Visit her. Let her tell you."

Then, without so much as a good-bye, Fairchild turned and walked off, leaving the man alone on the park bench where he clutched the new scrap of paper in one fist.

The man sat dumbfounded, staring after Fairchild as he disappeared into the distance. He looked down at the scrap of paper, and his irritation bubbled once again to the surface.

"You have got to be kidding me," he muttered.

He recognized the same handwriting on this note as on the first one—Fairchild's. This time, though, it contained only an address: "57 Waverly Street."

The man sighed and crammed the note in his pocket. Checking his watch, he felt the day's obligations once more closing in.

But instead of heading immediately back to his office, the man paused, slowly retrieved the wad of paper, and opened it again, wondering at the mystery it held.

❦   ❦   ❦

The woman opened the door halfway and stared out at the man. "May I help you?"

"Yes . . . I hope this isn't a bad time." The man held out his scrap of paper as if it were a passport. "A Mr. Fairchild suggested I should come and talk with you about your husband. I'm—"

"I know who you are." The woman stepped back and opened the door wide. "Mr. Fairchild called and said you were coming. Please come in."

The man entered the house, which was a comfortable mix of neat and messy, with the typical signs that children were alive and well, living in the home.

"Mark Fairchild was my husband's best friend." The woman waved the man toward the couch. "Please come into the living room and make yourself comfortable. Can I get you anything?"

"No, thank you."

The woman seemed relatively happy and peaceful, considering she was a new widow, the man thought, as he made his way to the sofa. He sat down, then looked around at all the evidence of family memories—photographs, children's artwork, other mementos. He turned toward the friend's widow. "I am so sorry that your husband has passed away. I'm sure he is greatly missed."

The woman nodded her appreciation.

The man continued. "Mr. Fairchild seemed to think that something extraordinary went on in this home. Since I make my living working with families, he apparently thought I might benefit somehow if I could talk with you a few minutes. Do you mind?"

The woman shook her head. "Not at all. What is it you want to know?"

The man shifted a bit uncomfortably. He was the one sent here. How did he know what he wanted to know?

"Well, I'm not exactly sure. As I said, this meeting was Mr. Fairchild's idea and ..." He cleared his throat, feeling out of control of the situation. His senses sharpened, though, as a result, a feeling he had not had in a long time. Finally he said, "Why don't you just tell me what happened?"

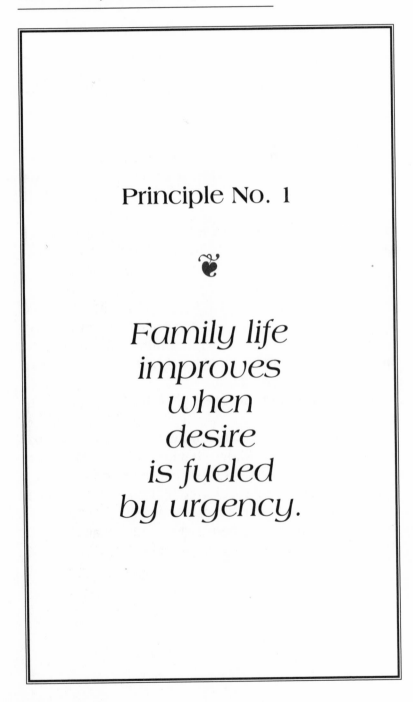

Principle No. 1

*Family life
improves
when
desire
is fueled
by urgency.*

The woman sat back in her armchair and closed her eyes for a moment. "It happened so fast. One second everything was normal. The next instant the doctor was telling me my husband had thirty days to live. It was like one of those before-and-after moments, you know? One minute life is as it's always been, the next minute life is changed forever and ever."

The man patted his pocket for a pen and a piece of paper. "Do you mind if I write down some of the things you tell me? I'm used to taking notes when people talk to me."

"No, of course not, go right ahead."

The woman shook her head as if to clear her mind. "The shock came in how quickly he got sick. He was in the hospital two weeks later in critical condition. We thought we were going to lose him right then."

"How long did your husband live?" the man asked.

The woman smiled. "He was told he had thirty days. That was it. From the very first hospital stay we were all mourning him as if he were already dead. Thirty days passed and he was still here. Then forty and forty-five. Sixty days passed and he was still here. It was hard to know how to feel." She paused. "He had stabilized, you see, and all of a sudden we realized he would be around longer than we thought. He hung on for nine months. Nine months . . ." She seemed to go off somewhere, and the man felt he was intruding simply by being there. Then she came back. "The last seven of those months were the richest and most fulfilling months my family has ever known."

The man stopped writing and looked up strangely at the wife. Then he realized she had noticed. "I'm sorry if I look surprised. It's been a long time since I have heard anyone describe their family as 'rich and fulfilling.' Given your circumstances, I am even more surprised to hear you say that."

The woman nodded, smiling almost wistfully. "I can understand your surprise. You had to have known my husband, what he was like before his illness, to appreciate how seven months, under decree of death, could be such a wonderful time. My husband loved his family, and, like most family men, he wanted to make us his priority, but it never really happened. Not until he found out he was dying. You see, sir—"

The woman stopped and bent close, so close the man could almost feel her intensity. "You see, my husband woke up one day viewing the rest of his life as thirty days and no more. Each month was his last. Do you understand? When that happens ..." Her voice trailed off, as if a memory had interrupted her thought. She began again, a quietness changing her face. "When that happens to you, everything looks different. An urgency most people find difficult to appreciate attaches itself to everything you do. Very quickly, you get deeply, mortally serious about the things that matter to you."

The man was impressed with her perspective. He studied the woman's face. He was an expert at studying faces. Yet hers was ... what? Strong? Knowing? Peaceful? Complete? He couldn't quite place it. He wondered how his own wife would talk if he were to die suddenly and she were having a similar conversation with a stranger. She would not be nearly so composed, he was sure.

He shook himself out of his thoughts. "Is that what your husband said? That he was very serious about things now that he was sick?"

"No, not at all," she corrected the man. "He knew he had no choice. He had this time and only this time to enjoy us. The effects of his illness came and went, sometimes hourly. During his good moments, he used to say he had gotten smart. He would shake his head at others who were seemingly oblivious to the gifts of life and love, after a while even calling them fools. My husband would say that people seemed to live as if they had all the time in the world, when the reality was that they were no better off than he was.

"'It's such a shame,' he'd say, 'that most of them will have to stare death in the face before they realize what they have. If only they could see with my eyes.'"

The woman glanced at a picture of her husband on the mantel, and her expression mellowed even more.

"When he decided to live his life thirty days at a time, he not only changed his life, he changed the life of every member of this family. Including mine. Do you have any idea what it is like to have someone you love focus his love on you as if he had only this month to do so? We all love others, sir, but rarely do we focus our love like that. We always believe there is time tomorrow. And if not tomorrow, definitely next month, after more pressing demands are met. But not my husband. That focus was transforming, and he did it, as I said, by living just thirty days at a time."

"What do you mean 'thirty days at a time'?" the man asked, scribbling quickly. "How did he live thirty days at a time?"

She grew quiet. "He made a point to use every one of his days the best he could," she said finally. "It's not difficult. I'll give you an example."

She smiled. "Early on, he had me bring him notebooks, one for each of the children and one for me. He ripped out all but thirty pages from each—thirty pages for thirty days. Then on each of the thirty pages, he wrote down one thing he planned to do for that person each day, to strengthen that relationship. Oh, they weren't big things, usually. I remember one day he wrote me a poem, telling me how much I meant to him. By poetry standards, it wasn't great. But to me, it was a precious gift."

The wife cocked her head, remembering. "Another day he very deliberately asked me to write down on a sheet of paper my worst fears about his dying and leaving me alone. I filled a whole sheet with my fears and tears. When I showed them to him, we spent an hour of uninterrupted time together crying—and strangely, even laughing—over everything I'd listed."

The man, writing furiously now, stopped and looked up expectantly, waiting for more. "Please go on."

But the wife only smiled softly, then suddenly stood up. "I'm afraid you will have to move on to get the rest of the story." She walked over to her desk and retrieved yet another piece of scrap paper and handed it to the man. "Mr. Fairchild wants me to send you to see my husband's sister for more answers to your questions."

The man sat speechless, looking down at another address in the now familiar handwriting: "Joan Milstead, 777 Main Street."

Seeing that the wife had finished all she wanted to say to him, he mumbled his thanks, clumsily put his pen and paper away, and followed her to the door.

The man stood for a moment in front of the woman's home. He was irritated again, if only slightly ruefully this time, because he was also intensely curious.

Mr. Fairchild had constructed his plan well, the man thought. How could he not now go to the sister's house and find out the rest of the story?

As the man walked toward his car, he noticed a cardinal singing in a tree. The observation surprised the man. It had been a long time since he remembered paying attention to such a thing.

❧ ❧ ❧

"Ma'am?" the man said to the woman on the other side of the screen door. "Your sister-in-law sent me over to talk with you. It's about your brother . . ."

The sister, like her brother's wife earlier, seemed unusually hospitable. She swung open the door and invited him, a stranger, into her house.

"Come in," she said. "My sister-in-law called and said you were on your way over. If you don't mind, let's talk in the kitchen while I finish up some work I am doing that can't wait."

The man followed her into the kitchen and found no place to sit. The sister was in the middle of a wallpapering job.

"I was moved by the story of your brother," the man began. "His wife described to me how much things changed for him when he started to see his life through a thirty-day window. Did you see the same changes?"

The sister balanced on the third step of the ladder and stretched a piece of wallpaper above the window.

"Absolutely," the sister said over her shoulder. "I have never seen a person more intense, in such a positive way. And I knew my brother well."

She stepped down from the ladder, and, wiping her hands on her jeans, she faced the man. "And it wasn't just that he was intense. It was as if he had a different focus, as if he were seeing things he hadn't seen before. For years, my brother's life had seemed so cluttered."

The sister rolled out a new piece of wallpaper. "Here, hold this for me, will you?" She reached for a scissors. "Thanks."

The man liked the sister—talking so frankly with half-hung wallpaper, dirty plates in the sink, coloring books on the kitchen table, and kids playing out back. He wasn't surprised to hear her speak of "focus." She seemed very balanced herself.

"My brother was pretty successful in the way we typically define success—you know, in his business and in his community. He had a whole lot of stuff going on. Then he found out he was going to die and going to die very soon.

"But after thirty days, when he realized he might have a bit of time after all, he decided he'd wasted thirty days. It was like an about face—no, more of a wake-up call. Anything can be done in thirty days, when you think it's all the time you've got.

"So he began making a big deal of living only thirty days ahead. He kept saying during those last months that he was discovering the hidden treasure in his life. That intensity, urgency, caused him to rearrange a lot of his priorities." She turned and began to smooth the wallpaper over the wall.

The man searched for his pen and paper. "Rearrange what?" he asked. "How?"

Principle No. 2

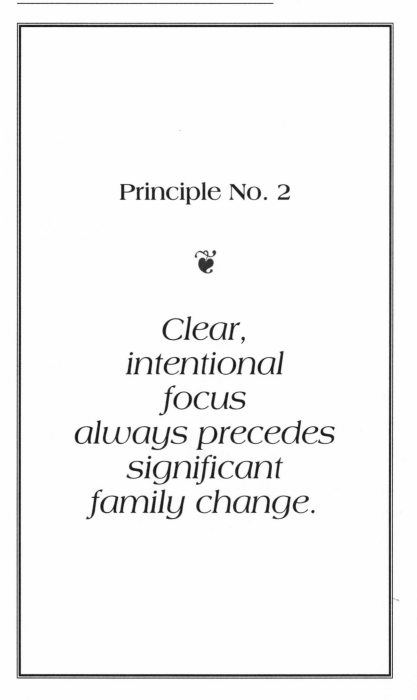

Clear, intentional focus always precedes significant family change.

The sister stopped her smoothing for a moment and stared off into space. "My brother had a lot of unresolved family business. He didn't have a good relationship with his in-laws. He was having trouble communicating with his teenager. You know, a lot of the typical stuff.

"Well, he went after each challenge like a tiger," she went on, "looking at each relationship as though he only had thirty days to fix it. He was really on borrowed time, you see, after those first thirty 'wasted' days."

She shook her head, smiling. "You know, he and my husband never really got along. There was always friction between them. I don't know why. They are—were—both wonderful guys. But one day, I showed up at the hospital and saw a notebook on my brother's table with my husband's name on it. My brother had decided he wanted to improve his relationship with my husband before he died. So for thirty days, each day, he made my husband a priority. Called him at work. Dropped him a note. Sketched out an idea for his business. When my brother died, no one wept harder than my husband."

She paused, a sweet, melancholy moment of silence. "We watched him turn a lot of things around. Quickly. He turned us around, too."

The man looked up from his notes to the sister. "How did he turn you around?" he asked.

The woman stared into space and then became quite serious. "My husband and I were like most people. We had a list of things we wanted to change, things we wanted to have happen for our family. Yet we'd carried these desires around for years and years, keeping them no more than desires. Because we had time. There was the usual amount of urgency, but not the kind that looming death brings, do you see? We found ourselves examining everything in a new way. What made us think we had more time than my brother did? Why weren't we experiencing life the same way as he was? We had no guarantee of time. Suddenly, we both were asking my brother's question—seriously— then acting on it, not just talking about it."

The man stopped writing. "And what exactly is the question he asked?"

"The best way I can answer that is to say what it came to mean for us: 'What if we had only thirty days left to do what we most want to do? What is really important to us? What do we want to do about it?'" She stopped to look straight at the man. "And you know what? It has transformed our family."

The man realized that this story had already begun to affect him. For the first time in so very long, he was interested in a family story. A seemingly unique one.

Could it be?

Standing there in that strange house, talking to a woman he had just met, all he wanted was to know what these people had found, what secrets had indeed so clearly transformed these families.

"But ... how was your family transformed? How do you do ... this?"

The woman laughed. "Do you have a family?" she suddenly asked the man.

"Yes, I do," he answered.

She pointed past the man out the window, into the backyard.

The man looked and saw someone he assumed to be the sister's husband with some children putting up a tent. The man checked his watch. It was the middle of the day, in the middle of the work week.

"He's the one you want to talk to," said the sister. "Let him tell you how we went about it. Wait here."

The sister walked out the back door.

The man watched through the window as she walked up behind her husband, who was pulling some guide ropes tight from the tent, and whispered something in his ear. The husband looked up and glanced back at the house, nodding. He said something to the kids and walked back toward the house with his wife.

The husband extended his hand to the man as the sister made the introductions. "Sir, this is my husband," the sister said. "I don't believe I caught your name."

"I'm sorry, I didn't give it," the man said. " My name is—"

"Let's go to the den and sit down," the husband interrupted, as if time was ticking away and there was a tent waiting to be finished. "Did you know my brother-in-law?"

The man looked the husband up and down. He was about two inches taller than the man and probably in his early forties. He seemed pleasant enough. But he was about to waste no time.

Principle No. 3

❧

*Time,
lovingly
invested,
shapes
the destiny
of
your family.*

"No, I didn't have the pleasure," said the man. "It's becoming obvious that I missed something. He must have been quite a guy. Your wife was just telling me about the unusual focus he gave to the last months of his life, how it rubbed off on all of you, and what a difference it has made in your own family. When I asked her how it had made a difference, she went to get you."

At that point, the man looked around and discovered that the sister had slipped back to her work. Now he was alone with the husband in the den.

That made the man feel a bit uncomfortable. Here was a fellow who should be at work, and yet he was playing in the backyard with his kids. This hit too close to home. He couldn't help but wonder if the sister's husband had calculated how much this nice afternoon at home was costing him in income. Yet the man had the distinct impression that this was not a particularly unusual afternoon.

The husband frowned, one eyebrow up, and looked at the man quizzically. "Does this interest you, really?" he asked. "I would think you'd have many better things to do. Most people do."

Now the man was very uncomfortable. "As a matter of fact, I don't. I work with families professionally, and I have one of my own that is very important to me. I am always looking for good pieces of advice that I can use both in my work and in my own home."

The husband walked over to the window to look outside at the kids playing. "Okay. Well, then, I'll give you a piece of advice."

He continued staring out the window. "I'll tell you the same thing my brother-in-law whispered to me seven days before he died."

He turned and faced the man now, and the man saw why he had looked away so long. The husband's eyes were rimmed with tears.

"Do you know what he said?" the husband went on. "He said, 'I found the key. The key is time. Your currency is time. It's the only thing we have to invest that we can control.' He said that was the most valuable thing he could tell me, something he did not realize until he was told he had only a little bit of it left."

The husband paused, as if to allow his words to sink in and his emotions to become steady again.

Then he added the rest as if it were the most important part: "Don't wait. Find time for what is important to you. Those dreams, those relationships don't happen unless you invest rock-solid time in them."

The husband looked outside and waved at the kids. "You know what?" he asked. "I've heard that a million times before, but until I saw my brother-in-law manage the last thirty days of his life, I didn't realize how important, how right it is."

He turned to face the man again. "Do you know how many times I tucked my kids in before my brother-in-law died? Maybe five times. How many times I called my parents? The last time I bought my wife a gift just because I loved her? The last time I made an effort to repair a bad relationship with any of my brothers or sisters? I don't remember when. Now I live my life thirty days at a time and invest my moments like the currency that they are. Nothing has been the same since."

With that, he cocked his chin high and nodded, as if reaffirming a truth to himself. "My wife is right," he said, strongly. "Her brother has transformed our home."

The man had forgotten to write anything for the last few minutes.

Why?

Because he kept thinking that all of it was almost too simple and too profound to be true. Could a person actually make such vast changes as these people were claiming by changing something so simple?

"What happened when you understood the importance of your time and how you managed it?" the man asked.

Before the husband could answer, the sister appeared in the doorway holding something very familiar by now.

Another piece of scrap paper.

"For the answer to that question, kind sir, you must pay a visit to my brother's eldest daughter, as I've been instructed to tell you. Here is her address."

Outside, after he had said his good-byes and thank-yous, with the children's laughter in the background, the man stopped and looked at the piece of paper: "Mary Smith, 40 Oaklawn Ln."

He refolded the scrap and placed it in his wallet for safekeeping. Then, for no reason he could explain, he took out the photos of his wife and children, something he had not done in a long time. He looked hard at them and was shocked to find that they were severely out of date—his teenage daughter's was a grade-school shot; his junior high son's, a T-ball photo.

He had no current pictures of the people he loved best in the world. He didn't much like what that said about him.

❦   ❦   ❦

The man rang the doorbell of the address on his scrap of paper for a second time.

No one was home.

He had used up almost his entire day chasing down this story. Hitting a dead end before he found out how this whole, unusual saga would conclude upset him more than he cared to admit.

He reached into his pocket and began to scribble his name and phone number on a piece of paper to leave in the door ... when he heard a voice behind him.

"May I help you?"

The man turned to see an attractive woman in her early twenties who held a small bag of groceries and was walking up the sidewalk.

She was very pregnant.

The man felt a bit flustered, not knowing where to start. "Yes, well, early this afternoon I met with a Mr. Fairchild ..."

The young woman seemed relieved. "Oh, you're the man Mother called me about. Let me get my keys out and you can come on inside."

The man glanced around. "I tell you what," he said. "Why don't you go on inside with your groceries, then come back out here, and we can sit on your porch? You don't know me, and I think you will feel a bit safer if we just sit outside."

She smiled at the man. "You're right. I appreciate your concern for me. Be right out." And she slipped inside.

The man sat down heavily on the porch. Nobody had told him the guy's daughter was pregnant. How many crazy turns could one story take?

He had a suspicion, though, that her condition was one of the reasons he was here.

"Can I get you anything?" the young woman asked him through the screen door.

"Just a few minutes of your time," the man answered.

The young woman walked out onto the porch and tossed a pillow down on the step. "That's for me to sit on. Don't move. I'm going to lean on your shoulder to get down there."

"I'm sorry," the man said. "We can go sit on those chairs over there."

"No, it's fine here on the porch. It's just a little difficult getting up and down. I'm due in five weeks. But I like talking about my father."

The man looked at the young woman and smiled. "Your father must have been quite a guy."

She cupped her chin in one hand and returned his smile. "He was. Especially at the end. He was a good father all through my life, but suddenly, last year, he became the best father anyone could ever have." She patted her stomach. "You can bet I paid close attention to what Daddy was saying during those last months. His granddaughter is going to have a better mother because of what he taught me."

The man reached into his pocket for his pen and paper. "I talked with your mother," he said, "as well as your aunt and uncle a little earlier. They told me about the 'hidden treasure' your father found by living his life thirty days at a time. Your aunt and uncle seem to have discovered the same thing. And your uncle was, well, quite emotional about the need to manage time and invest it wisely. Is that what you're talking about? Is that what you learned from your father?"

She nodded. "Mostly, but there is one more thing I learned that will help me continue the magic. During those last few months, every thirty days my father made himself write down what he wanted to see happen in regard to each one of us over the upcoming month. He wanted to know that if he died in thirty days, he wouldn't leave any unfinished business."

"Like what?" the man asked.

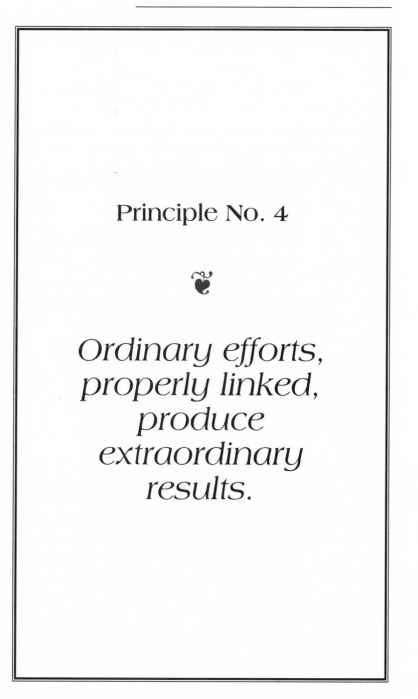

Principle No. 4

Ordinary efforts,
properly linked,
produce
extraordinary
results.

"Simple, small things. Ordinary things like maybe a phone call or a note.

"But," she went on, smiling even bigger, "when strung together thirty days in a row—well, I'm living proof that they produced some pretty spectacular results."

The man asked, "Sort of like a time-management thing?"

The young woman paused and then nodded. "Except this was very intentional and not very complicated. His list just focused on something happening every day with each of us in the family that he was in control of—instead of letting our family happen by accident. It was really something special, while at the same time so unbelievably simple."

The man paused. "Please, if you would—if it's not too personal—I'd like to hear one of those simple things."

The daughter looked away, shy for an instant, then laughed. "Okay. Here's one. Each day when I visited him in his hospital room, I'd catch him with his nose in one of our notebooks. When he saw me, he'd put it down hurriedly, and give me a smile. One time when I walked in, I remember him flipping it aside and saying, 'C'mere, sweetie pie.' You know what he wanted to do?" She pointed to places all over her face as her eyes filled with tears. "One more time he wanted to kiss me all over, like he used to do when I was little. I can't tell you how much I loved him in that moment."

She stopped for an instant, then, "Another visit, he took the time to hide in my purse a note he'd written. He said I was the joy of his life. And you know what?" She smiled. "I knew I was.

"You see," she continued, "it wasn't like my daddy and I were best friends or anything. But he made me important while he was dying. I fell in love with my daddy all over again. And you know what happened? After a while, all of us got our own notebooks, ripped out all but thirty pages, and started working at making each family member just as important as he did." She paused while the man scribbled. "Don't misunderstand," she hastened to add. "What happened—what he did and now what we are doing—is not a list of how-tos. The change happened because my father took responsibility for his love in the family. A love that cared enough to create a plan of loving and then live it." The daughter stopped and looked directly at the man. "Live it as if there were no tomorrow."

She paused. "You know, it's funny. Even though Daddy was dying, our family was better those last months than when he had all the time in the world. One day at a time for thirty days." She patted her stomach again and smiled. "That's how I'm raising this one—thirty days at a time."

"Well," the man said, putting away his pen and paper. "Thank you very much. I need to get back to my office. Let me help you up." He stood up, reached for the young woman's hand, and helped her to her feet.

"Thank you for stopping by," she said. "As I mentioned, I always love the chance to talk about Daddy." She walked across the porch and opened the door to go inside.

The man was lost in his thoughts as he descended her porch steps. It was an extraordinary story, yes. What everyone had told him made sense, and, at the same time, what they'd said was frightening. Did a person have to be under a sentence of death to see so clearly?

How could he ever hope to feel the same sense of urgency that had seemed to lift this dying father and husband to new heights with those he loved? How could anyone? It could mean so much, could change so many families, but was it even possible for the average family not in the throes of such tragedy?

Behind him on the porch he heard the screen door slam shut once again, and the daughter's voice call out to him. "Oh, by the way," she said, "I had a message from Mr. Fairchild on my answering machine. He wanted you to call him after you finished talking with me."

Ah, yes, Mr. Fairchild, the man thought as he continued down the porch steps. I want to speak to him, too.

But then the man looked at his watch, sighed, and began walking briskly toward his office. "He'll have to wait," the man muttered aloud. "I've got so many other things I must do today after all this running around."

❦   ❦   ❦

When the man returned to his office, his secretary stood up as he came through the door. "There is a man who insisted on waiting for you in your office," she told him. "I don't know who he is or what he wants."

The man smiled, shaking his head. "Ah, but I bet I do," he said as he went into his office. "Mr. Fairchild, greetings!" the man said, closing his door behind him. "I was going to call you as soon as I had the chance." He moved around behind his desk. "I have a lot of questions. I've got some things I have to do, though, before . . ."

What he saw as he turned to face Mr. Fairchild shocked him so much that he couldn't finish his sentence. Mr. Fairchild's face was pale, much more so than when they had met earlier just that afternoon. Obviously something was wrong. Very wrong.

"Mr. Fairchild! Do you need to lie down?"

Mr. Fairchild waved the idea away impatiently with a strained cough. "Did you see everyone?" he wanted to know. His voice, so firm and confident just this morning, was now raspy and faint.

Trying not to let Mr. Fairchild's appearance distract him, the man pulled his notes out of his coat pocket.

"Well, I think so. That was quite an adventure you sent me on. Everyone had so much to—"

Mr. Fairchild rose from his chair in the middle of the man's sentence, and the man reached out for Fairchild's hand to help steady him.

But Fairchild grabbed the man's forearm instead, urgently, pointedly. "Listen to me," Fairchild said. "I didn't send you on any adventure." He coughed, hard this time.

It was obvious that whatever was wrong was getting worse by the moment.

"What you heard today," explained Fairchild, "I heard twelve months ago when my friend died. I listened to the same story you did. I thought the same thing you're thinking. I felt the idea a good one, something I should try to do when I had the time to think it through.

"And nothing changed in my life all this time. Nothing! I just kept going along, frustrated because I couldn't find the 'big' amount of time to plan even the smallest things that needed to happen to give me a family like his. I wanted to, oh, I wanted to. My sons, my wife, I needed to do so much with them, for them. I could see it. But I didn't change a thing!

"And now it's my turn—now I'm the one who has run out of time . . ." Fairchild coughed again. He released the man's forearm and slumped into the chair.

"Sue, call an ambulance, quick!" the man called to his secretary. He ran around his desk toward Fairchild. "Mr. Fairchild, are you all right?"

"No, I'm not," Fairchild said, grimacing. "Forgive me for this. I thought, as always, I had time. I thought I had the time to talk to you before another attack today. But they're coming more frequently now. This will pass, and then there'll be another, and soon it will be constant, no time left at all, you see. So you must listen." Fairchild strained to lean toward the man. "I chose you. I chose you to hear the whole story, including my part. Do you understand?"

Fairchild turned his head to cough again. "Don't be deceived like I was. I look at my family, and I am upset I didn't act. You are no different. The people who come to this office are no different. I thought you, of all people, might hear me, might take the story to heart and do something, tell others what I knew and what I could have done. So people won't keep making the same mistake."

Then Fairchild reached out, grabbed the man's hand, pressed a piece of paper into it, and lay his head back into the chair, his strength gone.

The paramedics arrived. They rushed Fairchild out of the man's office, leaving the man and his secretary standing in shock at the dramatic scene that had played out before them on this unusual day.

The sound of the siren moving off in the distance was a signal, somehow, to turn back to the affairs of the day. The man sat down heavily behind his desk, still too stunned to speak.

He opened his hand to reveal this one last scrap of paper Fairchild had pressed there. This time, scrawled on it was a personal note. The message read: "Your journey to the family of your dreams never starts tomorrow."

Principle No. 5

Your journey
to the
family
of your dreams
never
starts
tomorrow.

The man looked up, feeling his face flush. Something very significant had happened to him that day. He knew it in his bones.

The man grabbed his coat and rushed out his office door. The secretary looked up just as he flew by her desk.

"Sue," he told her, "reschedule the rest of my sessions and take messages for me the rest of the day. I have to go home."

"Are you all right?" she called after him.

"Starting now, Sue," he called over his shoulder, "starting right now, I am going to schedule important things for my todays."

The secretary frowned, trying to recall a time when she had detected more urgency in the doctor's voice.

No, she thought to herself. She was sure she never had.

❦ ❦ ❦

The man stood quietly over Fairchild's grave.

He was alone now; the family and friends who had attended the funeral had left.

He reached into his pocket, pulled out a card, and set it against the headstone. Then, laying his hand on the grave marker for a silent moment, he moved on.

The card stayed upright for a moment, then it flapped loose in the fall breeze and blew across the grass to land against the leg of a groundskeeper.

Glancing down, the groundskeeper stopped his work to scoop it up.

And this is what he read:

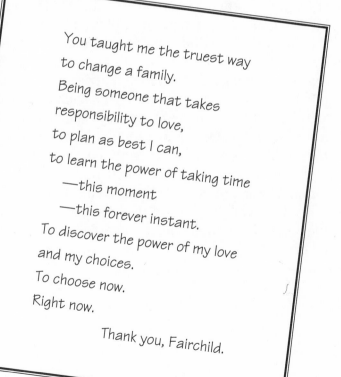

You taught me the truest way
to change a family.
Being someone that takes
responsibility to love,
to plan as best I can,
to learn the power of taking time
—this moment
—this forever instant.
To discover the power of my love
and my choices.
To choose now.
Right now.

Thank you, Fairchild.

Epilogue

The story you have just read is based in part on a true story. It happened to a friend of ours. On December 30, 1995, Thom received a phone call from Richard Johnson, the director of the College of Child Development for Family University and one of Thom's closest friends. Richard told Thom that he had returned that day from the doctor's office with the shocking news that he had terminal cancer.

Richard Johnson died thirty days later, leaving behind a wonderful wife, an incredible daughter, and many friends. And much of what happened in those last thirty days transformed his family and the lives of those around him, including ours. Sometimes, in the scheme of things, thirty days is all you get. What we have written are some of the things we learned from our dear friend in the hope that all of us will have much more.

Part II

❦

The Next 30 Days

Certainly you are smarter than Fairchild. Now that you know what the man learned, you won't make the same mistake. Before another day passes, get ready to turn your desire for a smarter family into action. So let's get started.

Grab a pen or pencil. The next few pages provide the tips you need to take the first step right now. As you read the story, no doubt you thought of one or two areas in your family relationship that you'd like to improve. Before you forget, write a couple of words or phrases here that identify the projects you are thinking about.

Did you write down…

• the name of a family member with whom you want a better relationship *(a child, a spouse, a grandparent, an aunt or uncle, an in-law)*?

• a habit in your family that needs to be started or replaced *(better communication, honest communication, controlled TV viewing, promptness, money management, more praise and appreciation)*?

• a difficult change in your family circumstances *(a death, a divorce, the arrival of a new baby, loss of a job)*?

• a dream for your family that you've carried in your heart for a long time *(new family traditions, spiritual growth, a specific hobby or involvement in a service activity, more time for reading, travel)*?

Whatever your concerns might be, look at your list and select one item as your family project for the next thirty days. This project—your blue ribbon—will be your first step in the journey to a smart family.

❦ ❦ ❦

Above the blue-ribbon "target" on the next page, write the words or phrases that identify your goal. In the ring around the bull's-eye, write some statements that describe in detail the changes in activity or behavior that would have to occur for you to know you've reached the goal.

For example, if better family or marital communication is your goal, the statements written in the ring might be: "Everyone in our family can freely express their true feelings. My views and ideas are valued. My style of communicating is understood and accepted. We work through our differences and negotiate our conflicts instead of avoiding them."

Be as specific as you can about how the situation will look when your goal is reached.

30-Day Project: _____

_____

_____

❦   ❦   ❦

Now think of some specific steps or activities that will help you reach your stated goal. Imagine these as being like the shaft of an arrow that will carry the tip (your desire for a smart family) to the center of your family target. Below the arrow shown here, list these steps and activities.

If your goal is better family communication, action steps or activities might be things like: ■ Identify a daily or weekly time to talk as a family or couple. ■ Practice

Activities which will help

Guiding principles and beliefs

"reflective listening." ■ Avoid put-downs and quick, judgmental responses. ■ Minimize interruptions by turning off the TV or phone during meals or important conversations. ■ Call home when you are running late or your plans change. ■ Make five positive remarks for every negative comment.

Inside the arrow feathers at the left, write some guiding principles upon which you will base your actions: *Treat others the way I want to be treated. Forgive and forget mistakes. Love without conditions.*

us reach our goal

❦   ❦   ❦

Next, follow the example of the man in the story as he wrote in his notebooks. Begin assigning the activities and steps to specific weeks and times over the next thirty days. Try first to establish a flow, using the sections below to distribute your steps throughout the next four weeks. Then, using the spaces on pages 78 and 79, assign very specific and simple actions to each of the thirty days on your calendar. Remember Principle 5: "Your journey to the family of your dreams never starts tomorrow."

Week One

• _____
  _____
• _____
  _____
• *(Weekend)* _____

Week Two

• _____
  _____
• _____
  _____
• *(Weekend)* _____

Week Three

• _____
  _____
• _____
  _____
• *(Weekend)* _____

Week Four

• _____
  _____
• _____
  _____
• *(Weekend)* _____

List below extra ideas or random thoughts that could contribute to reaching your 30-day goal. Don't worry if you aren't yet sure about how to use them. The columns at right and on the next page offer a variety of action tips that might stimulate your thinking.

_____

_____

_____

_____

_____

_____

_____

_____

_____

_____

_____

_____

_____

_____

_____

_____

_____

_____

_____

_____

_____

_____

_____

_____

_____

Some helpful tips ...

· As much as possible, get everyone involved in setting goals and planning action steps. That way everyone owns the plan.

· Leave spontaneous notes at school or home, and make surprise phone calls during the day to work or home. These have especially high impact because they interrupt routines. Use them often to cheerlead and remind each other about your 30-day project.

· When you need an hour or more to talk and work through some parts of your project or carry out a task together, find the time. Turn off the phone, go to an isolated part of your home, retreat to the back booth in a restaurant, or maybe sit in the car. Give smaller kids a coloring book or a similar "quiet" activity to keep them busy while older family members talk.

· Whenever conflict or tension arises over how to proceed, don't force things. Stop. Say you are sorry and take another approach. Talk, and work through issues only as long as you can do so calmly. If that's not possible, try again later.

Some more tips . . .

- "One bite at a time"— that's the fabled best way to eat an elephant. It is also the best way to provoke family change.

- These questions can help you sort your "good ideas" from your "great ideas."

  - Of all the ideas so far, which best meet our needs?

  - Which ideas could help us "win big," not just "get by"?

  - Which ideas best fit our family's style and personality?

  - What facts need to be uncovered before we can properly decide?

  - What are the good and bad side effects to the ideas we are considering?

  - Is the timing right?

  - What should or could we stop doing to take on this new project?

- If your family calendar is already jam-packed, set aside any optional activity to focus attention on this special 30-day project.

- Hug and touch more than usual as you move through the 30 days. Most of us need more hugs.

🐞 🐞 🐞

*I*t is important to visualize your goals and celebrate your progress along the way during your thirty-day adventure. Everybody needs to be clear about the specific steps for this week and the goal for this month. And everybody loves the encouragement of "high fives"—those compliments and pats on the back—especially from other family members.

Use every opportunity to praise the good work someone does, notice important changes made, reward new habits, and build teamwork within your family. In fact, anticipate when a celebration would be especially appropriate and reserve the date on your calendar.

*T*ry making a simple triangle-shaped "table topper" (like the one sketched here) to set on your breakfast table. It will remind each family member about your mission during the thirty days and the specific steps you are working on this week. Put hand-made signs (note the ideas across the page) and Post-It notes around the house to remind and encourage one another about the goal. Add a balloon from time to time and maybe a paper streamer, just to make it more fun and festive. Building a smart family is big-time stuff and you should celebrate it in the same way you celebrate birthdays, anniversaries, and other important family events.

Organize and list here the specific activities and actions you will take on each of the next thirty days. Then transfer them to your daily calendar.

Our Next 30 Days

Principle 4: "Ordinary efforts, properly linked, produce extraordinary results."

1. _____

2. _____

3. _____

4. _____

5. _____

6. _____

7. _____

8. _____

9. _____

10. _____

11. _____

12. _____

13. _____

14. _____

Think Smart

15. _____
_____
16. _____
_____
17. _____
_____
18. _____
_____
19. _____
_____
20. _____
_____
21. _____
_____
22. _____
_____
23. _____
_____
24. _____
_____
25. _____
_____
26. _____
_____
27. _____
_____
28. _____
_____
29. _____
_____
30. _____
_____

Think Smart

❦   ❦   ❦

We have designed a series of guidebooks to help you and your family regularly work smarter to solve a family problem or to grow in a particular area of family life . . . thirty days at a time. One of these guides is Part III of this book—Communicating Value. It offers a thirty-day plan for building your family by learning how to more effectively express appreciation to each other. Research on family strengths consistently documents that expressing appreciation is one of the hallmarks of a strong family.

We encourage you to decide now on a time to begin this thirty-day project to strengthen your family's appreciation skills. Or, select from one of the other three guidebooks announced at the back of this book. They are available separately. Whichever topic you choose, it is important to seize this golden moment and get started now!

Part III

Communicating Value
Building Your Family
by Expressing Appreciation

Project Overview: *Communicating Value*

30 DAYS to a SMART FAMILY

Day 1	Day 2	Day 3
What Mirror?	The Heart of Appreciation	The Fruits of Appreciation
Part I: Finding Focus		

Day 8	Day 9	Day 10
Crushing Criticism	Moon Shots	What Do We Need? **Time-Out!**
Part II: Clearing Hurdles *(cont.)*		FAMILY MEETING

Day 15	Day 16	Day 17
Great Choices	Appreciation Accounts **Time-Out!**	Word Power
Part III: *(cont.)*	FAMILY MEETING	

Day 22	Day 23	Day 24
The Feelings Detective	Mistaken Gifts	Good and Angry
Part IV: *(cont.)*	**Part V: Making Appreciation a Habit**	

Day 29	Day 30	
Through Grateful Eyes	We Can Appreciate Clearly Now **Time-Out!**	
Part V: *(cont.)*	FAMILY MEETING	

Day 4	Day 5	Day 6	Day 7
ppreciation vs. Flattery	Prospecting for Gold Time-Out! FAMILY MEETING	A Weak Foundation	Gifts Out of Control
		Part II: Clearing Hurdles	

Day 11	Day 12	Day 13	Day 14
ome Climate Control Time-Out! ILY MEETING	Doin' What Comes Naturally	Character Strengths	Home Work
	Part III: What to Appreciate		

Day 18	Day 19	Day 20	Day 21
26 Mighty Soldiers	You've Got the Touch	Giving an Eyeful	I Caught You!
Part IV: How to Appreciate			

Day 25	Day 26	Day 27	Day 28
Encourage Me!	Very Rewarding	Appreciating Younger Children	Appreciating Older Children
Part V: Making Appreciation a Habit			

Introduction
Verbal Dynamite!

I can live for two months on one good compliment.
—*Mark Twain*

*I*t is virtually impossible to overstate the positive impact of regularly expressing appreciation to one another in the family unit. Time and again, studies of strong families reveal that *affirming* one another is a basic cohesive factor in every truly happy family.

If you have decided to focus on building your marriage and family life by expressing more appreciation as your first *30 Days to a Smart Family* project, congratulations! You have made a wise and perceptive choice.

The fruits of your efforts will multiply themselves for weeks, months, and years to come—even into the next generation. Receiving sincere words of appreciation, especially at home, can feel like breathing pure air in a world of pollution.

How to Use Part III

Part III is a guidebook designed to help you and your family take a step each day of one entire month toward learning to express appreciation. These insights and activities will help you practice regular affirmation in your relationships.

Each day introduces an insight *(something "To Think About")* and suggests a simple activity or application exercise *(something "To Do")*. Each daily step can easily fit into a busy schedule. If you miss a day or two or more, don't become discouraged. Pick up where you left off and keep going. Before long, you will have formed new habits and will be enjoying all the expressions of appreciation as they are exchanged in your home. Don't let anything sidetrack these thirty important days of family development.

In some families, gaining the attention and cooperation of certain family members can be a challenge. They may not initially see the deep value of the project. Fortunately, developing and practicing appreciation skills can begin effectively with you alone. Others will join in as their attention is captured; your fresh words and deeds of appreciation will motivate them. Modeling is a powerful way to teach.

Nothing is so precious as your family. Fairchild finally understood this, but it was too late. Fortunately, you now realize that today is the best time to get started.

Part I: Finding Focus

What Mirror?

Affirming words from moms and dads are like light switches. Speak a word of affirmation at the right moment in a child's life, and it's like lighting up a whole roomful of possibilities.
— *Gary Smalley and John Trent*

🍎 **TO THINK ABOUT:** Like it or not, words have an awesome ability to build us up or tear us down. This is particularly true within the family. You can probably remember clearly words of praise your parents spoke years ago. More likely, you can recall negative and cutting words directed at you by someone in the past. The setting and the speaker's facial expression may still be vividly etched in your memory.

A new high school student-council president included the statement, "My dad believes in me" in his acceptance speech. After attempting suicide, another student quipped, "My parents think I'm stupid." Each statement uses just five words, but what a contrast. One breeds life, the other death.

How did these young people acquire such deeply motivating views of themselves and their abilities? They were shaped by "mirrors" held up to them by their parents. A parent's words become a mirror—revealing to the child either a positive or negative view.

Only the most misguided parents would intentionally ruin a child's self-esteem. But it can easily happen if the parent fails to realize that he or she is the one upon whom the child depends to put life events—both ups and downs—into perspective. Mom and Dad's daily unguarded words and actions establish the meaning of such occurrences.

Kids crave parental approval. They look into a parent's eyes for clues about how well they are doing. A parent has the opportunity to immortalize moments in a child's life. Authors Gary Smalley and John Trent express it this way: "It takes a loving, attentive parent to take a common stone (event or experience) and turn it into a milestone in a son's or daughter's life."

❧ **To Do:** Close your eyes for a moment and reflect on the mirror your parents (and other significant adults) held in front of you. Jot down the positive and negative feedback that still rings in your ears:

Positive words spoken to me:	*Negative words spoken to me:*
_____	_____
_____	_____
_____	_____
_____	_____
_____	_____
_____	_____

Make tally marks below for each positive and negative comment you can remember making to your child over the past week or two. Be honest.

Positive remarks:	*Negative remarks:*

Ponder your answers to these questions over the next twenty-four hours. If you have a spouse, compare your answers.

Part I: Finding Focus

The Heart of Appreciation

*The deepest principle of human nature is the craving
to be appreciated.*

—*William James*

❦ **To Think About:** Affirming and appreciating others involves ascribing value to them: uplifting them, extolling, magnifying, and honoring them; commending them and applauding the content of their heart, as revealed in their words and deeds.

True appreciation in the family looks beyond each member's faults and mistakes to celebrate all that is unique and special about that person—affirming his or her distinctive place in your heart. The focus is on the positive. As Matthew Fox observes, "Healthy families remind each other of their goodness; unhealthy families remind each other of their failings."

In your family, appreciation that counts cannot be manipulative—an insincere tool to get what you want, to squeeze out a little more performance from the kids or to keep control of a relationship. True appreciation is the kind that is genuinely expressed from one person's heart to the heart of another.

❥ **To Do:** We all develop habitual ways of seeing and treating others in our family. Sometimes these views aren't entirely fair and need adjustment. Try one of these exercises to accent the positive and renew your perception of one another.

- Create an acrostic using the letters of each family member's first name. Then use each letter to begin a word or phrase that describes one of that person's positive qualities. No negatives allowed.

- At bedtime, pile everyone on a bed with a bottle and something hard to spin it on. Play a new version of "spin the bottle." The one who spins the bottle must identify a quality he or she admires in the person the bottle points to. Then that person spins, and so forth.

Part I: Finding Focus

The Fruits of Appreciation

*The best families I see are those in which members
care enough about each other to give a sense
of support and self-esteem. The kids know
they're worthwhile because the family
makes them worthwhile.*

—*A pediatrician*

❧ **To Think About:** M. Scott Peck tells us where a child's self-esteem originates in his classic, *The Road Less Traveled:* "Children who are truly loved, unconditionally, know themselves to be valued. This knowledge is worth more than gold ... The feeling of being valuable—I am a valuable person—is essential to mental health and is a cornerstone of self-discipline. It is a direct product of parental love."

High self-esteem is universally understood to be the foundation of healthy living and relationships. Defined simply, *"self-esteem is the sense of being lovable and capable."* In the mirror created by words and actions in the family, children see a reflection that they believe to be the truest picture of who they are. Frequently expressed appreciation makes this reflection vividly positive.

- Communication flows more freely.
- Inter-dependency is energized.
- Growth and maturity is encouraged.
- Potentials for taking risks and for achievement are liberated.

The result is that children and spouses believe they are valuable, loved, and capable of reaching the full potential of their gifts and abilities.

❥ To Do: Spend ten minutes today in a quiet place. Close your eyes and picture your child standing in front of you. Imagine a video cassette recorder between your child's eyes and ears. Everything the child hears and sees and feels is recorded into the VCR. Ask yourself: Who is the big star in this movie? Recognize that the answer is . . . you! Are you satisfied with your starring performance? Where would most of your remarks or actions fall on the axis of parental feedback?

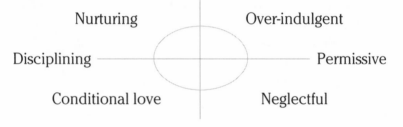

Affirming

Nurturing   Over-indulgent

Disciplining ——————————————— Permissive

Conditional love   Neglectful

Unaffirming

Note: The feedback you received as a child and your own personality type both strongly influence your instincts as a parent. You will tend to lean toward one of the quadrants more than another. On any given day or week, however, your feedback may not fit your norm. Simply study these two axis continuums and the four parenting results long enough to grasp the general dynamics.

Part I: Finding Focus

Appreciation vs. Flattery

Good words are worth much and cost little.
—*George Herbert*

🍂 **To Think About:** While both flattery and the expression of appreciation accentuates the positive, we can draw a subtle distinction between them. **Appreciation statements** typically begin with the word "I" and acknowledge the value in a person's deed or action. The focus is on what was done or said. For example:

- "I appreciate your thoughtfulness and effort."
- "I appreciate the help, Peter. You didn't miss a thing when you folded that laundry and put it away. I couldn't have done it any better myself."

The more specific the appreciation being appreciated, the more powerful the impact.

Flattery statements, on the other hand, typically begin with the word, "you" and draw attention to the person, instead of to the person's deeds. For example: "*You* are wonderful, *you* are great, *you* are outstanding." This kind of general praise can backfire if a child starts thinking: "Yeah, right! If you really knew me, or what I'm thinking right now, you wouldn't have said that."

Flattery can lead others (especially children) to believe that their worth stems mostly from how they measure up to what the speaker expects or wants.

Appreciation gives children or adults the assurance that their value will be the same whether they succeed or fail in the deeds they attempt. This promotes honest effort

and growth. Performance pressure is not a factor. As family specialist Kevin Lehman says about honest expressions
or appreciation, "This leaves them [children] free to
always try, without fear of being criticized, scolded, or
expected to jump a little higher next time."

Flattery says, "You're great because you did something." Appreciation says, "It's great that something was
done, and I appreciate you for it."

❥ **To Do:** Set a goal this week to make at least one appreciation statement to each family member every day. (Follow the example of the dying man in the story and fill a
thirty-page notebook with simple ways appreciation can
be expressed—one a day to each family member.) Focus
on personal strengths. This will affirm each person's feelings of capability and build positive self-esteem. Look for
opportunities to express, in front of another adult, your
appreciation for your child.

List below each family member's name and one of his
or her routine deeds or actions for which you are grateful
this week:

_____ : _____

(Person)

_____ : _____

(Person)

_____ : _____

(Person)

_____ : _____

(Person)

_____ : _____

(Person)

Time-Out!

Prospecting for Gold

*Children are developed the same way Carnegie
explained that gold is mined: Tons of dirt have to be
removed to get an ounce of gold. But you don't go into
the mine looking for the dirt. You go in looking for the gold.*
—*Paul Lewis*

DAY 5

This *30 Days to a Smart Family* project is designed to involve every family member.
Use your time today to help draw everyone in—especially that spouse or older child who may have been away or who has not yet expressed interest in this project.

For a few minutes after dinner or at bedtime, hold a brief family meeting. At that time ...

- explain why you want to become better at expressing appreciation.

- take the following Family Appreciation Quiz. (Ask each family member to answer true, false, or usually.)

T F U

__ __ __ 1. In this family, we freely compliment and praise each other.

__ __ __ 2. In our family, when a child talks, as much attention is paid as when an adult talks.

__ __ __ 3. I believe (child's name) _____ feels appreciated by me as a parent.

__ __ __ 4. The children in this family express appreciation for what the parents say and do.

__ __ __ 5. We give praise when a family member loses as well as when he or she wins.

__ __ __ 6. The atmosphere in our family is one which encourages us.

- Describe how you hope a special focus on appreciation skills will make your home a happier place thirty days from now and how your relationships and interactive patterns will be different.
- Suggest that each family member try to help the others break the bad habit of unrestrained criticism.

Tip: When you realize insensitive and negative words have slipped out of your mouth, stop yourself and say, "Cancel" or "I'm sorry! I didn't want to say that!" or "Let me say that differently." You might even say to your child, "I just realized that I've been using words that hurt me when I was little and I don't want to do that anymore. The next time you hear me say that, please remind me."

When hurt by your words, your child might want to communicate with you using specific signal words: "Replay," "Cancel," or "Ouch, Dad, try again."

Remember: Success is picking yourself up one more time than you have fallen down.

On the Appreciation Bookmark No. 1, at the back of this section, is a pledge to participate in this thirty-day project. Ask each family member who agrees, to sign it. Clip it out and place it in your day planner or in another place you can regularly refer to it. It also lists the topics to be covered over the next four days in Part II, "Clearing Hurdles." As a reminder, jot in the day of the week you plan to tackle each hurdle.

Part II: Clearing Hurdles

A Weak Foundation

The Golden Rule of Parenting: *Do unto your children as you wish your parents had done unto you!*

🌳 **To Think About:** Elementary school teachers can tell which of their students live in emotionally healthy homes. Positives and negatives experienced at home show up in the classroom big-time!

Stephanie Marston, author of The Magic of Encouragement, tells about a mother who stood in the kitchen and lashed out at her daughter, "What a pig! You never put anything away." Suddenly she was dumbstruck as she realized that the very words she hated as a child and had sworn never to utter were the very words she was spewing forth in tones of righteous indignation at her daughter. Like many parents, she was unaware that she was replaying old childhood tapes for her own child's ears. You may have experienced this too!

You need positive self-esteem in yourself. In order to grow in your ability to express appreciation to others, you must be able to value yourself, to treat yourself with love, dignity, and respect. To possess high self-esteem is to feel that the world is a better place because we are in it. We radiate a sense of trust and hope. Integrity, honesty, love, and compassion flow freely from those who have high self-worth.

🔖 **To Do:** It takes uncommon self-awareness to diagnose one's own esteem deficit, and real courage to tackle its repair. If low self-esteem makes it difficult for you to consistently appreciate others, try some helpful self-talk when such feelings tear at you. Repeat in your mind a carefully crafted and truthful statement about yourself such as, "I am an intelligent, caring, and worthwhile person and/or spouse, acting with responsible love and maturity toward my family. " A professional counselor can assist you in dealing with deeper self-esteem problems.

Share your own stories and ask others in your family to recall times when they felt good about themselves. Examine what they were doing and who they were with at those times. Recite as much detail as possible. Which of the following situations can you recall?

- I felt important to someone I respected and whose opinion I valued.
- I felt I did something that only I could have done in that particular way. I felt special and had a sense of my own unique gifts.
- I felt in charge, accomplishing something I had set out to do. I felt confident that I could handle any problem I might face.
- I shared a difficult-to-express thought, feeling, or opinion with someone. In doing so, I connected with that person on a deeper level than ever before.*

A strong antidote to a child's low self-esteem is immediate, frequent, and positive encounters with important people in that child's life.

---

* From *The Magic of Encouragement* by Stephanie Marston (New York: William Morrow & Company, Inc., 1990).

Part II: Clearing Hurdles

Gifts Out of Control

*The unrestrained passion of natural abilities is the
greatest threat to a healthy, adult life.*

—Thom Black

🐦 **TO THINK ABOUT:** Throughout our lives,
mistakes and failures are brought to our attention far more often than accomplishments and
successes. On school papers and tests the
wrong answers are highlighted, not the *right* ones. At a
job performance review the employer might offer a few
positive words, but most of the attention is focused on
areas needing improvement.

This kind of corrective feedback (the opposite of
appreciation) overlooks a critical insight. Most of our
behavioral mistakes—errors in self-control, judgment, or
timing—are connected to one of our strongest personal
abilities or gifts. That character trait that caused us to err
is the same one that enables us to do our best work; the
ability was simply used in a negative or harmful way.

For example, some individuals have a natural gift for
leadership. During their lifetime, these people make supe-
rior contributions to the organizations they serve. However, while this gift may have been active during their
childhood, it wasn't yet developed and was not under
their control.

In the contest of will between parent and child, a child
who is a natural-born leader doesn't want to be told what
to do. He or she is forever trying to direct household decisions. Due to immaturity, however, the child frequently
goes about this in unacceptable or disrespectful ways.

In reaction, the parent disciplines the child's willfulness, unaware it is being fueled by one or more of the child's deepest and most natural gifts—the very ones a caring parent wants most to value and appreciate. To every gift and strong ability, there is always a dark side.

The same issue affects you as a parent. One of your strong abilities may be to quickly size up a situation, to speak with powerful words, or to express compassion. Maybe you are good at being a star or at organizing activities. When this gift gets out of control, however, you may not be able to adapt it to a family situation. Instead of looking for something to appreciate in your child at that moment, your first instinct is to use your gift to control the situation.

❥ To Do: Stand back and be objective for a few minutes. Think of some recent times your child exhibited negative behavior and try to identify the natural abilities and character strengths you might have missed. As you see these abilities and strengths acted out over and over in a variety of settings, begin to express your words of appreciation. Your positive words will sink deep into the heart of your child.

Even as you discipline your child for negative behavior, try to remember to comment on the underlying positive ability that was momentarily out of control—the good intentions behind the behavior—and the good things you know will happen in the future as your child matures and becomes better able to control his or her great strengths.

Part II: Clearing Hurdles
Crushing Criticism

Kids absorb criticism like a sponge.
—*Stephanie Marston*

❦ **To Think About:** A study of parent/child interaction by the National Parent-Teachers Organization determined that the ratio of critical responses to praise responses was an average of 18 to 1. A study at the University of Calgary showed that verbal abuse is even more likely to damage a child's self-esteem than is physical abuse because children evaluate themselves by their parents' opinions. Unchecked criticism is a verbal poison that can deeply erode our relationship with our kids.We know how difficult it can be to correct our children's behavioral mistakes and remember to affirm them at the same time—especially during emotionally charged moments.

One effective and essential key in responding to our children is to separate the child from the undesirable behavior. "You" statements ("You can't do anything right." "What's wrong with you?" "How could you be so stupid?") focus on *who the child is* (which he or she *cannot* change) rather than on *what the child does* (which he or she *can* change).

When we use "you" and follow it up with a noun or an adjective that we feel describes the child, we pass judgment on the child, not on their behavior.

"I" statements are more effective in accomplishing the goal: "I feel _____ when you _____ because _____ , and I want you to _____ ." *

* "Owning your feelings" is a technique made popular by Dr. Thomas Gordon in his book *Parent Effectiveness Training.*

(I feel angry when you leave your shoes on the living room floor because they make the room look messy, and I want you to put them in your closet.") "I" statements work because they (1) are specific, (2) focus on the behavior and not the person, (3) clearly let your child know what you *do* want, and (4) emphasize the cause-and-effect relationship between the child's actions and your response. "Mom feels _____ because I did _____ ." Judgment skills are learned in this way.

Substitution is another means of responding to negative behavior: "Don't do _____ ; do _____ instead." ("Don't hit your sister; hit a pillow or your punching bag, instead.")

Please note that not all "you" statements are damaging.

- "You did a good job."
- "You need to finish putting away the dishes."
- "You must be proud of yourself."

Your tone of voice alerts your child to the type of message you are sending.

❧ To Do: Take a pencil and mark an "x" on the line below at the point which you believe fairly represents the balance between the "you" statements and "I" statements you usually make to your child.

You	*I*
statements	*statements*

Now, if you want to be sure you are in touch with reality, ask your children for an opinion about this. Explain the difference between "you" statements and "I" statements. Then draw the above continuum on a paper and ask your child to place an "x" on the line. If a spouse is present, try the evaluation again.

If you are dissatisfied with the responses you and your family members have given, you just discovered another reason why this project is important. Make a note on your calendar to retake this test again at the end of your thirty-day project.

Part II: Clearing Hurdles

Moon Shots

*A family is a group which possesses and implements an
irrational commitment to the well-being of its members.*
—*Dr. Urie Bronfenbrenner*

🐛 **To Think About:** Let's be honest. It is hard
to think appreciative thoughts about a child or
spouse when the person's behavioral quirks
have gotten on your nerves. We want to feel
daily appreciation for our loved ones, uncover new
golden nuggets to appreciate. However, we become discouraged by the tons of "dirt" we must first clear away.

At the same time, our children often feel caught. Our
expectations for them are so high, trying to meet them
feels like trying to reach the moon. Children easily
become discouraged as well. They soak up disappoint-
ment seen in our looks and heard in phrases we often
insensitively tack onto our sentences:

- "How many times have I told you . . . "
- "Surely you realize . . . "
- "When will you ever . . . "
- "If you had any brains . . . "
- "You always . . . "
- "You never . . . "

Sound or feel familiar? Let's hope not.

Take a moment to read Dr. Bronfenbrenner's statement again. The key word in his definition of family is
"irrational." It means that, even though you are disap-
pointed with a family member's choices or behavior, you
will still stand up for and believe in the person—looking
past the behavioral quirks that trouble you. It also means

that you can't affirm the person's actions, while you can affirm this person. Your love is unconditional. It's this irrational dimension of your love that really pays off.

❥ **To Do:** Keeping a sense of humor in the relationship between you and your child is essential. When you realize you have set your expectations too high, your child needs to see you laugh at yourself for making such a mistake. It helps relieve the embarrassment the child may feel over failing to meet your standards.

Today or tomorrow while driving with your child (or with the whole family) quote Dr. Bronfenbrenner's statement about family and ask, "What actions in our family show that we are irrationally committed to each other?" Think of one new way you can express such a commitment today or this week.

Time-Out! (A)

What Do We Need?

Parents need to fill a child's bucket of self-esteem
so full that the rest of the world can't poke
enough holes in it to drain it dry.

—Unknown

DAY 10

Too frequently our children get the message, both spoken and unspoken, that their worth is contingent upon staying out of trouble, being neat, doing well in school or music or sports, or an endless list of things that make parents proud. Could this be true in your family?

Get the whole family together today and tomorrow for some simple evaluation. Provide popcorn and sodas at a thirty-minute meeting today and take the following three steps:

Step One: Ask each person to identify the family member who best fits the following descriptions (it could even be a family pet):

This person gives me hugs.
This person is available to talk with.
This person is prompt.
This person believes in me.
This person expresses anger in a healthy way.
This person is a calming influence around the house.
This person gives compliments.
This person shares personal feelings.
This person helps me find solutions.
This person remembers special things I like.
This person greets me when I come home.
This person is generous.*

* From *Family is Still a Great Idea* by H. Norman Wright.

Step Two: Talk about the times over the past week (since your last family meeting) when you were able to correct yourself after making a discouraging remark to someone, or when you helped another family member recognize how a remark he or she made to you was hurtful. Clap, cheer, and whistle wildly in recognition of each successful moment.

Step Three: Form a big group hug and shout together three times: "Day by day, we are getting better at expressing appreciation." Hang a homemade paper banner in the kitchen this week, signed by each family member, which reads, "WHAT A FAMILY!"

Time-Out! (B)

Home Climate Control

*This is the hunger we all have—to be liked, to be
loved, to share our love and lives—yet many families
are unable to satisfy this hunger. For a variety of
reasons, they are unable to fulfill this deceptively
simple purpose for living together in a family.*
—*Delores Curran*

J ust as each person in your family possesses
one-of-a kind fingerprints, so the basic climate or mood of your family is also distinctive.
Family specialist Dr. Jerry M. Lewis explains that
this "mood" is the one on which the family operates when
all is going well. How your family survives its stresses
depends upon this basic mood. In some families, even
when all is going as well as can be expected, the basic
mood or climate is one of depression.

A hallmark of the mood in healthy families is hope—a
forward-looking quality. While some stresses may last for
years, they are viewed as temporary. A healthy family
always seems to dredge up the resources to deal with
them.

At a short follow-up family meeting today, check the
"emotional weather" patterns—the climate typically experienced in your family. Ask family members to talk about
times when the "weather" in your family relationships felt

- Sunny, with warm breezes
- Partly cloudy
- Overcast and cold
- Rainy with thunderstorms
- Windy, with a tornado watch

- Snowy, with blizzard-like conditions
- Cold and warm like a spring thaw with possible flooding

Now, let each family member suggest how the ways you treat each other can help create sunny days with warm breezes.

Ideas: Listening and talking, helping one another out, focusing on solutions instead of placing blame, taking time to play, planning surprises.

Over the next week, agree to set the climate control thermostat in your home on "sunny and warm breezes" by greeting each person in a positive way, especially during the first four or five minutes after everyone arrives home each day—whether from school or work, early or late. No griping or negative comments can be shared during that time. Instead, everyone will try to show interest and concern to each other (as well as share hugs and kisses).

Talk about the appreciation-expression insights you hope to develop over the next four days of this thirty-day family project as you look below at "What to Appreciate." Post a notice on the family bulletin board or refrigerator door that shows these topics for the next four days: (Next to each title, write the day of the week that topic will come up.)

What to Appreciate:

- Doin' What Comes Naturally - (day of week)
- Character Strengths - (day of week)
- Home Work - (day of week)
- Great Choices - (day of week)

On the Appreciation Bookmark No. 2, at the back of this section, write in the day of the week you will focus on each topic. As a reminder, clip it out and place it in your day planner or at another place you will see it regularly.

Part III: What to Appreciate

Doin' What Comes Naturally

*God has put something noble and good
into every heart his hand created.*
—*Mark Twain*

❧ **To Think About:** When expressing appreciation, our natural tendency is to focus on *what people do*: acts of kindness and support, or their various gifts—large and small. At a more foundational level, however, we need to value people just for *who they are*—for "being" as well as for "doing." We want the members of our family to know that they are loved, no matter what.

On Day 7 we looked at how our natural gifts, when out of control, generate behaviors that irritate and get us in trouble with other members of our family. However, looking beyond the irritation to notice and appreciate family members for their natural gifts is one of the most loving habits a family can acquire.

➥ **To Do:** As a family or individual activity, make a list of the behavior you see in each family member which (1) sometimes irritates you, (2) you've heard others comment on, and (3) has enabled that person to achieve good things.

Now look for the underlying "abilities" being used at these various times of irritation or success. For example (and there are many others), it might be that the person was basically

- interacting with and uniting people
- extracting the potential from a situation
- meeting the needs of others or a situation
- overcoming the challenge of a difficult moment

- gaining a response from people
- meeting the requirements of a situation

Focus your appreciation on these basic abilities. In this way you will be nurturing other family members just as a mother's milk nourishes a baby.

For example: A sibling who won't stop making an aggravating noise or who is always getting into your personal stuff (negative behaviors) is also demonstrating the ability to be resourceful and overcome challenges. A "workaholic" spouse may have strong entrepreneurial abilities (extracts potential) or managerial abilities (meets requirements) ... although they are out of control.

Part III: What to Appreciate
Character Strengths

I have a dream that my four children will one day live in a nation where they will not be judged by the color of their skin, but by the content of their character.
—*Dr. Martin Luther King Jr.*

❦ **To Think About:** Check one box: "My child ❏ has character; ❏ is a character." In all honesty, most parents would have to check both boxes. On Day 12 we focused on the "is a character" issues that merit regular appreciation and the underlying strengths they demonstrate. Today, our focus shifts to the "has character" strengths family members see in each other, qualities such as honesty, loyalty, faithfulness, humility, generosity, trustworthiness, compassion, reliability, teachableness, kindness, gentleness, helpfulness, fun, lovability, determination, and the like.

You can make a profound contribution to your child's growth, self-understanding, and maturity if you can help the child see that he or she has many unique, God-given attributes. These can be contributed in a classroom or group setting. These natural traits will attract people (when the child is not trying to be someone else instead). Constantly remind your child not to compare him- or herself to his or her brothers or sisters or anyone else. Always point your child back to his or her own unique gifts and abilities.

❧ **To Do:** Think about how you would answer the question: "Tell me about your [son, daughter, husband, wife, father or mother]." Most of us would spend a sentence or two describing physical features—especially something distinctive—then rather quickly switch to describing that person's personality traits and character.

As a family, make a list of the distinctive character qualities you can see in each other—traits like those listed above. Spend a few minutes flipping through your family album or box of photos. Select one or more snapshots that show these qualities in action. Sit down as a family or one-on-one. Show that family member the photo and describe the gift you see at work. Tell the person how much you value and appreciate this quality.

If photos aren't available, describe a picture you can imagine taking of that family member. What is the picture that would reflect the character strength you have in mind?

Have all family members select one character quality they would like to gain or enhance. Help each other think of one specific step to take or habit to work on this week, which would enhance growth in this area. Write it down on a 3x5 card and post it on the bathroom mirror or bulletin board as a reminder for the week. Note it also on your bookmark.

Part III: What to Appreciate
Home Work

*The object of love is not getting something you want, but
doing something for the well-being of the one you love.*
—*William James*

❦ To Think About: As we have observed earlier, when it comes to expressing appreciation, what usually comes to mind first are the tangible and intangible gifts others give us. Although the lion's share of these are probably given and received in the home between parents and children, home can also be the place where words of appreciation are heard the least— especially for the common and expected gifts: food, shelter and clothing, transportation, a stereo, and TV.

How do you think home life would change if suddenly the contributions made by each family member were to cease? What would suddenly be missing? What problems would this create for you?

➤ To Do: Write the name of each family member at the top of a piece of paper. Under the name, make two columns: title one "Physical Contributions," and the other "Emotional Contributions." Then brainstorm together what you should include on each person's list.

Under Physical Contributions be specific. Include everything from making beds and cleaning (floors, toilets, windows, cars, and clothing) to earning the money for food, electricity, trash pickup, the mortgage, birthday parties, meals out, soap, and toothpaste.

Under Emotional Contributions, list things like laughs a lot, listens well, comforts hurt feelings, loves, communicates with extended family members, stays up late waiting, creates care for the family, and makes music for the family.

Post these lists in a prominent place for a few days so that family members can add new items as they think of them. And as a reminder of the things you want to be sure to express appreciation for.

Part III: What to Appreciate
Great Choices

*Accept your child's strengths and weaknesses, flaws
and assets so he can learn to accept himself.*
—Cheri Fuller

🍏 **To Think About:** The power of choice is
basic to feeling alive as a human being and to
experiencing freedom. When this power is exer-
cised, it both rewards and hurts us. On the down

side, the power of choice is often what gets us into trouble
(and teaches us many of life's best lessons). As someone
observed, "To be a person who never makes a mistake, be
a person who never makes a decision."

On the up side, good choices powerfully reward us as
we see and experience the fruits, successes, and delights
resulting from good decisions. In your family, appreciating,
affirming, and celebrating everyone's good choices, and at
all different stages in life, provides an important contribution
to your mutual happiness, joy, and sense of well-being.

These choices are usually memorialized in our photo
albums and video clips of family members as they succeed in a sport or talent, complete another phase of their
education, or just stay alive long enough to celebrate
another birthday. Equally worthy of appreciation, but less
noticed, are the smaller, more daily and weekly choices
that are critical to reaching our larger successes.

➤ **To Do:** Just for fun, brainstorm together at the dinner
table or over a snack of popcorn about what would happen
if each family member stopped making good choices of the
daily and weekly kind. Suppose Dad or Mom no longer
stopped at stop signs, or were no longer nice to their friends

or boss, or to each other. Suppose you stopped taking regular showers, or failed to brush your teeth, or to eat enough protein, or to care for a pet. Add some real spice by telling about those times that in reality you made poor choices and what the outcomes were. Kids always enjoy knowing about the times Dad or Mom blew it.

Thank family members for doing the right thing and for setting good examples. Tell them how proud they make you feel to be a part of this family.

Make a decision to always express appreciation for the right choices you see family members and others make. You will be developing an excellent habit.

Time-Out!

Appreciation Accounts

Praise does wonders for our sense of hearing.
—*Arnold Glascow*

DAY
16

or about two weeks now we've focused on understanding the value of appreciation. Hasn't it become quite clear why expressing appreciation is one of the top characteristics researchers consistently find in strong families? Do you find yourself viewing other family members in a more positive light?

Imagine that each of you in the family has an account at the Bank of Appreciation. The larger the balance in your accounts, the "wealthier" you are as individuals and as a family, and, as with any account balance, it is important to monitor its status to make sure your balance is growing.

An account-balance check can be taken in less than five minutes. Close your eyes and think back over the past seven days. What are the "deposits" you can remember making in each family member's account? Count each *intentional* "deposit" on your fingers. Set a personal goal: you will make five or six specific deposits during a week's time.

If you fall short of that goal, or make large withdrawals in the form of harsh criticism, or if other "draining" negative experiences occur during the week, determine to improve your deposit-making during the following week.

The various ways to make deposits—the "how to" skills of expressing appreciation listed below—is our focus during the next six days of this thirty-day family project. It will be fun. Post a new sheet listing these topics on the bulletin board or refrigerator door so that everyone can anticipate the day each will come up. Or you could write them on a sheet of paper, fold it in thirds like a brochure and tape the ends together to form a table-top reminder for the kitchen table. (See the sketch on page 77 in Part II of this book.)

How to Appreciate skills:

- Word Power - (day of week)
- 26 Mighty Soldiers - (day of week)
- You've Got the Touch - (day of week)
- Giving an Eyeful - (day of week)
- I Caught You! - (day of week)
- The Feelings Detective - (day of week)

On Appreciation Bookmark No. 3, at the back of this section, note the day of the week you expect to work on each skill. As a planning reminder, clip it out and place it in your day planner or in another place you can refer to it regularly. Now, track your progress in planning and completing appreciation deposits in each skill area over the next six days.

Part IV: How to Appreciate
Word Power

*Your words are very powerful. They can evoke hostility
or happiness. They can fill your home with conflict or
with an atmosphere of loving support.*

—Paul Lewis

🌿 **To Think About:** We all experience seasons of self-doubt. During these times, do the negative and critical words expressed to you in the past, maybe even years ago, ring again in your ears? That's word power!

The apostle James described the power of words this way. He compared the tongue to the small "bit" placed in a horse's mouth. With it, this powerful animal is made to move in any direction the rider chooses. Similarly, James observes, it takes only a small rudder to turn a mighty ship in the ocean (see James 3:3–5). King Solomon, in his legendary wisdom, starkly described the power of words when he wrote, "Death and life are in the power of the tongue" (Prov. 18:21 KJV).

Consider this sobering question: "Do I treat my family as well as I treat my friends?" Actually, many of us would never say to a friend the harsh, demeaning words that escape our lips at home. The person wouldn't remain our friend.

"Empty talk" describes many of the words spoken within families. There is a lot of talk, but little is said, and even less is done. When our words are not thoughtful and well-focused, or when they reveal that we've not been paying attention or listening to the other person, our words lose their value. Our spouse or our kids turn a deaf ear and tune us out.

"Maintenance talk" also plagues many homes. We pass in the hallways and rooms, greeting each other with only a grunt. Customary "How are you?" and "How was your day?" questions are asked at the dinner table. Checking questions are frequent: "Did you pick up your toys? Take out the trash?" Or, "Mom, where's my skateboard?" Everyone talks, but the content isn't significant.

❥ **To Do:** Determine that beginning today, you will improve your ability to express appreciation, using clear and powerful language. Try these three approaches:

1. Use word pictures to freshen your appreciation vocabulary and impact: "You took to _____ , like a _____ to _____ ." "I don't think _____ himself, could have done a finer job than you just did." "Watching you brings to mind your [grandfather, uncle, nephew], 'The Great _____.' You are going to be every bit as accomplished at _____ as he was." Describe your love and appreciation for younger children in gigantic terms: "bigger than the ocean, higher than the sky, etc."

2. Begin regularly asking family members to give you their opinion about things—news stories you hear, decisions you are trying to make, or maybe about the activities of sports figures or media stars. When you hear a fresh viewpoint or thoughtful reflection, express appreciation by commenting, "That's an interesting/insightful comment. I've never thought about it that way before. You've really challenged my thinking."

3. Think back on past achievements family members have experienced. Practice expressing appreciation verbally by recalling that success: "Remember that time you _____. I may not have said so then, but I was quite impressed by the ability you demonstrated to _____ . You were awesome!"

Use the first ten minutes in the morning as your kids wake up and the last ten minutes at night before they fall asleep to load them up with appreciation messages. These times of day are a child's most emotionally open moments. The first launches good feelings about themselves as they start their day. The second allows their subconscious to play your appreciation messages over and over all through the night.

Write on your bookmark planning guide the verbal deposit(s) you will make.

Part IV: How to Appreciate

26 Mighty Soldiers

Good words are worth much and cost little.
—*George Herbert*

🌱 **To Think About:** Those twenty-six letters of the alphabet you learned as a child—twenty-six "soldiers" capable of fighting off self-doubt and making your child's heart sing—are some of your best weapons in the daily battle to express appreciation. Spoken words may not be remembered for long. But when written down, those same words can repeat your message over and over again for weeks—even throughout a lifetime.

Stephanie Marston took ten minutes to write her daughter this note following a difficult period the child experienced at school: "Ama, I really feel good about the way you handled yourself and the situations with Wendy. I love you. You're very special to me. I'm glad you are my daughter. Love, Mom." The note meant a great deal to Ama. She put it in her special box where she keeps her good memories.

One dad always put a positive note in his daughter's lunch bag each day. Later he discovered that she had papered the whole back of her bedroom door with his notes.

You don't have to be a professional writer to create written appreciation that has punch. The only requirement is that your words come from the heart and are consistent with your other actions.

🍴 **To Do:** Here are a number of fresh ideas that will enhance your written appreciation style:

1. As you go through your day and find yourself thinking often about a certain family member, jot a short note to that person, not a reminder list of "to do's," but a list of things you appreciate.

2. Write love notes to serve your child for breakfast, or slip a note under your child's bedroom door. This is an especially helpful idea when you must leave the house before your child is awake.

3. When you visit your child's school classroom during an open house night, leave behind a note praising your child's work. If you can't be at open house, or the science fair, or the game, slip by the school beforehand and leave a note expressing your admiration.

4. Blow up a balloon and hold the air in long enough to write an appreciation message on it with a marker pen. Then let it deflate and enclose the balloon in a card or put it somewhere else your child will find it.

5. When you send your child to a friend's house overnight, or to camp for a week, or off to college, enclose a special pillowcase on which you and other family members have written expressions of your love and appreciation. This reminder can feel mighty good on a "homesick" night.

Choose one written appreciation idea that you will "deposit" in a family member's account today. Write this plan on your bookmark.

Part IV: How to Appreciate
You've Got the Touch

The point is not to do remarkable things, but to do ordinary
things with the conviction of their immense importance.
—*Teilhard de Chardin*

🍎 **To Think About:** Could it be true that in
many homes, the family pet receives more frequent strokes and hugs than the people do?
Actually, this is possible, particularly if the
kids are teenagers; although teens still need to be
touched—just in different ways than when they were
youngsters. Healthy touch helps a parent's spoken and
written words sink in. It makes them more believable.
Physical contact between people is one of the most
basic expressions of trust.

Family cultures vary with how much physical affection
is "normal." Fathers especially can become confused about
how to appropriately touch a child, especially a daughter,
who appears to be an adult but who is emotionally much
younger.

Research suggests that it takes four hugs a day for sur-
vival, eight for maintenance, and sixteen for emotional
growth. A parent can provide many comforts and opportunities for a child, but there is no greater reassurance of
lovability and worth than to affectionately touch and hold
your child—and while you're at it, include kisses,
squeezes, cuddles, and pats on the back.

Dr. Harold Voth, senior psychiatrist at the Menninger
Foundation, says, "Hugging is an excellent tonic. Hugging
breathes new life into a tired body and makes you feel
younger and more vibrant. In the home, daily hugging will
strengthen relationships and significantly reduce friction."

♣ To Do: Touch and hug each other more than ever before! Try foot rubs, back rubs, and head massages, pats on the back, wrestling on the floor, and light contact games and sports.

Tender touching is sometimes a forgotten skill. Sometimes we are more tender toward our animals, gardens, cars, and jewelry than we are toward our spouse and children. As you set a child's breakfast in front of him, squeeze his shoulder or hand. Rub her shoulders or the back of her neck as you help with a homework problem. Give a gentle pat as you pass in the hallway. Such small gestures say, "I'm glad you are here."

In a cultural climate where physical and sexual abuse are at all time highs, simply ask your child from time to time whether any of the ways you touch him or her make the child feel uncomfortable. Explain that you want your child to feel completely loved, but never uncomfortable in any way with expressions of touch.

Using touch, what will be your appreciation "deposit" today? Note your plans on your bookmark.

Part IV: How to Appreciate
Giving An Eyeful

*When was the last time you looked into your child's
eyes? Are they still brown? Are they still big? Do you
know how to say "I love you" to your child
by the way you look at him or her?*
—*Thom Black*

🐞 **To Think About:** The verbal part of communication is only a portion of the total message
—by some estimates less than thirty percent.
Hours, days, or just minutes after you speak, the
actual words used may not be remembered, but the feelings and nonverbals conveyed are often unforgettable.
The impact of our communication is much more powerful when our body language and emotions are in sync
with our words.

Eye contact and facial expressions, in particular,
communicate volumes to a child almost instantly. No
caring parents can afford to miss entering through their
child's eye gate. Positive eye contact is an unsurpassed
way to say, "I'm paying attention to you." "I care." "I want
to know you." "I love you!" The eyes are often called "the
window of the soul."

🌶 **To Do:** At a mealtime or bedtime today (or during a
family bull session), talk about and demonstrate the
"looks" you can remember catching as a child from your
dad, mom, teacher, neighbor, or relative. Tell what they
meant and how they made you feel.

Encourage your child to talk about your own parental
"looks" and how they make him or her feel. Can your child
mimic your various "looks"? Laughing together at the effort can relieve tensions and create a healthy moment.

Should you discover that your "looks" are sending messages you do not intend, quickly make the necessary adjustments.

Make an appreciation deposit using eye contact and a kind look today. Note your success on your bookmark.

Part IV: How to Appreciate

I Caught You!

*Kids will never stop trying for a father or mother
who thinks they're the greatest.*

—Unknown

❦ **TO THINK ABOUT:** None of us likes to be discovered doing something wrong. Catching our kids "in the act," however, seems to go with the territory of parenting. But catching them in the act doesn't always have to be a negative. How about catching them in the act of doing something right? Instead of your child feeling shame and the urge to hide, he or she will feel pride and the warm glow of parental approval.

Getting good at positive "catching" takes practice—we've done it the other way for so long. As parents, most of us are far better (and certainly quicker) at pointing out a child's failures. But it doesn't take long to realize that something is wrong with this picture. If my child's positive accomplishments don't receive at least equal billing with the mistakes, chances are my child will lose interest and become discouraged over his or her human frailties, instead of enthralled with his or her human potential.

We need to put on imaginary parenting "glasses" that filter out our instinct to be critical first and to praise later. We must to see more clearly the potential our "great expectations" will unleash. Catch your child doing chores without being reminded, speaking with kindness to a sibling, being helpful, practicing a sports or musical skill, going the extra mile on homework, sharing an insightful thought or observation, making the family laugh, even catching him- or herself before a wrong choice is made.

When we believe in our children's potential, our kids begin to believe in it as well. They hear us talking frequently about our belief in them. Such genuine words of potential, spoken against a backdrop of unconditional love, tend to become self-fulfilling prophecies. We are our child's cheerleader.

❧ To Do: Find or take one or more snapshots of your child doing "the right thing." Make sure the child's facial expression clearly reflects his or her delight. Mount this photo, along with another of the whole family, at eye level next to the child's bed. What greets him or her first thing in the morning and is the last thing seen before falling asleep at night is him- or herself as a successful person, belonging to a loving family.

Stephanie Marston recommends frequent "Star for an Evening" nights where one child "star" receives the family's undivided attention. This can be during dinner or an after-dinner show-and-tell time. During this time the child is urged to talk about accomplishments, special activities, and whatever is most interesting to him or her. At the end, stand and give an ovation of applause, cheers, hoots, and whistles. Such special times foster feelings of closeness, satisfaction, and enhanced self-esteem.

Note on your project bookmark each family member you "caught in the act" and what "the act" was. Tell the whole family about it.

Part IV: How to Appreciate
The Feelings Detective

*We all become more beautiful when we are loved, and
if you have self-love, then you are always beautiful.*
—Alice Walker in The Color Purple

🐛 **To Think About:** In her book, *The Magic of
Encouragement*, Stephanie Marston explains that
most us grew up in homes where the existence
and intensity of our feelings was denied. Conse-
quently we heard statements like "You've no reason to be
upset," "It can't be that bad," or "You're making a moun-
tain out of a molehill." Such disregard for the place of
emotions makes it harder for us to respond emphatically
to our kids. Yet developing healthy emotional patterns is
critical to a child feeling loved and capable—the two
components of self-esteem.

Parents as well as children must learn to understand
communication on a feeling level, and become good at
managing feelings. Kay Kuzma puts feelings in perspective with her pyramid diagram of the four levels of
communication—from *clichéing* on the lowest level, to
reporting, to *thinking,* then to *feeling* on the highest level.
It is essential that children, regardless of gender, have
the opportunity to express all of their emotions. Children
can't help what they feel. Feelings are neutral—neither
right nor wrong. You can accept a child's feelings without accepting a child's behavior, but there is definitely
a connection between feelings and actions. The way we
help children learn to manage their feelings is to listen
to and accept their feelings.

(Sharing your deepest feelings. Appropriate only when you are deeply committed to each other.)

(Expressing your thoughts and beliefs. "I think ... ")

(Relaying the "facts" of the day. "A funny thing happened ... ")

(No-risk statements or questions. "How are you?" "Fine.")

❥ To Do: Reflective listening—being "a feeling detective"—is one of the simplest and most powerful ways to acknowledge a family member's feelings. When we deny our children their feelings, or declare that they should change their feelings, these feelings don't go away. They get bottled up. And bottled up feelings just become stronger, eventually errupting as tantrums, hitting, bad dreams, and so on.

When a child is upset, you can show empathy through understanding verbal feedback. This will help the child begin to understand his or her feelings, as well as provide time for the feelings to dissipate and be worked out in constructive ways. Stephanie Marston illustrates how such a conversation might unfold:

Mom: "Stephen, how was your day?"
Stephen: "Lousy. I hate Chuck and Jason."
Mom: "You sound upset."
Stephen: "I mean it. I hate their guts."
Mom: "Something must have happened to upset you so."
Stephen: "It did. They ran off, and I had to walk home myself."
Mom: "I bet you felt hurt and left out."

Stephen: "I did. I'd like to punch them in the nose."

Mom: "You're really annoyed with them, aren't you?"

Stephen: "Yeah. I'd like to throw them in the garbage."

Mom: "Gee, you seem really angry with them."

Pair off in your family, then think back to a recent upsetting moment and role play the exchange of conversation between you and your child. Practicing this will help both of you. Take turns being the angry person and the empathetic listener until your words flow comfortably. Now you are ready for the next time hurt feelings erupt.

Stephanie relates what one son told his mom after she began to acknowledge his feelings: "You've always been on my case. Now, you're on my team." And remember, empathizing with the feeling does not mean you are condoning the behavior.

Note on your bookmark the times you have had a "feelings" dialogue with a family member.

Part V: Making Appreciation a Habit

Mistaken Gifts

*We really can't enjoy life until we learn how to see and
say something positive about everything.*
—*Charlie "Tremendous" Jones*

❦ **To Think About:** Besides death and taxes,
one more certainty is always with us—mistakes!
The fruits of our poor decisions, large and small,
constantly play themselves out in our lives and
the lives of our children. Our mistakes can become our
greatest teachers when we are able to receive as a "gift"
the insights about life and its choices.

Valuing the opportunity for personal growth presented
by these unwelcome tutors is another habit of appreciation both we and our children can cultivate. Appreciating
the silver lining in mistakes involves giving empathetic
feedback when a child blows it, not filling the air with "I
told you so's" and angry lectures.

An angry response to your child's error strips away the
more useful focus on the lesson to be learned from the
mistake's logical or natural consequences. It gives your
child an out by allowing him or her to react to your anger
instead of dealing with the consequences of the mistake.

A far more valuable response to a child's mistake is
your expression of sadness—a genuine sorrow for the mistake that was made—and empathy amid the confusion or
ugly feelings the child may be experiencing.

❧ **To Do:** You can prepare to respond to your child's
next mistake by practicing saying some "empathy" phrases
to use in place of getting angry. Here are some effective

ones from the authors of *Love and Logic*. Write them on a card and carry it with you today:

- "What a bummer!"
- "Really? I know you, and no mistake is going to get you down. I'm sure you'll come up with something."
- "That's terrible. How are you going to handle it? There must be a lesson to appreciate in there somewhere."
- "Hm-m-m, that's a really interesting way to look at it. Let me know how it turns out."
- "Oh, no, I'm glad that's not my paper [report card, grade, late assignment, specific problem, etc.]. You must feel awful. What can you do?"

Comments like these keep you squarely on your child's side of the problem and thus in a good position to encourage him or her to look past the frustration to the insight or lesson to be learned and ultimately appreciated.

Helping your child find the words to clearly explain the difficulty a mistake has created is an important first step toward helping the child find the best solution.

Part V: Making Appreciation a Habit

Good and Angry

A torn jacket is soon mended; but hard words
bruise the heart of a child.

—*Unknown*

🍎 **To Think About:** Affirmation and anger would seem to be at opposite ends of the emotional spectrum. In terms of typical outcomes, they are. One strengthens the bond between individuals, the other alienates. Within the family, however, affirmation and anger are joined at the hip in a couple of strategic ways.

First, when properly expressed, anger can affirm love. Often we hide angry feelings for fear of saying or doing something abusive. The purpose of expressing anger is not to make the other person feel bad; rather, it is to clarify the underlying cause of the anger. Anger is almost always a secondary emotion triggered by hurt, frustration, or fear. Identifying that hurt, frustration, or fear helps you begin to deal with the underlying cause—the fact that you care and are not indifferent to the other person's pain.

Second, when properly used, anger can create a doorway for solving a problem or improving a relationship. Management is vital to keep anger from tearing down what affirmation has built up. When family members realize how much their words or actions have offended or hurt you—evidenced by the intensity of your emotion—their love can begin to create new actions and words that will build rather than tear at the relationship. Stuffing your anger actually communicates that you are indifferent to the family member's behavior—exactly the opposite of

139

what you want to communicate. Learn to say, "I wouldn't feel so hurt or frustrated if I didn't care for you so much; if I didn't want so much for this [parent/child or marriage] relationship to work."

❦ To Do: Answer the questions: "Has anger ever produced a positive result in our family? Why or why not?" It can by taking these steps:

Step One: Admit and accept responsibility for your anger. The other person or situation didn't put the anger into you. (It's not true that "He made me so angry.") The family member just provoked a situation that revealed your capacity to get angry.

Step Two: Recognize the warning signs—a tensing of your body, a faster heart beat, louder or faster talking. Learning your "anger pattern" is the beginning of anger management.

Step Three: Gain control. Give yourself a few moments to calm down so you can think clearly. That way, the words you say will teach rather than tear down. "I feel angry because I became hurt [frustrated, fearful] by what you just did [said] to me. I need you to _____ ."

Step Four: Forgive each other. Appreciate each other for valuing the relationship enough to work through the problem instead of hiding from it. And always look for a way to turn an insensitive remark around. When, in frustration, one mom called her son "A little Twirp," she redeemed her comment quickly by explaining that from now on a "twirp" in their family would mean a totally awesome, irresistible, responsible person.

Part V: Making Appreciation a Habit

So Encourage Me!

*No one, great or obscure, is untouched by genuine
appreciation. We have a double necessity: to be
commended and to know how to commend.*

—Fulton Oursler

❦ **To Think About:** One of the largest reasons
we fail to be appreciative is also the simplest—
we can't think of the appropriate words. This is
no excuse, of course, but being at a loss for
words stops us long enough that the opportune moment
passes us by. This isn't a problem for talkative individuals,
but the quiet or reserved parent or family member can
benefit from some practical help.

➤ **To Do:** Spend a few extra minutes tonight around the
dinner table with your family, or even around the lunch
room table with your coworkers, recalling and brain-
storming the various ways and phrases you can think of to
express appreciation and encouragement.

Determine to replace the words *won't, can't,* and *that's
wrong* with phrases like *you can do it, you're improving,*
and *let's take a look at the problem.*

Answer these questions to get you started:

• Recall past words of encouragement or appreciation
that meant a lot when spoken to you.

_____

_____

_____

_____

_____

_____

_____

_____

_____

_____

_____

_____

_____

_____

- List here the words that mean a lot to your kids and that they would love to hear more often.

_____

_____

_____

_____

_____

_____

_____

_____

_____

_____

_____

_____

_____

- List on the next page phrases you have found to be effective. To get you started, consider these: "Good job! I appreciate your efforts to ... " "That's it! You're on the

right track for sure." "Your room [or whatever] looks ter-
rific. You didn't miss a thing. Thank you!" "I'm happy seeing you enjoy your work. I'll bet you're happy too ... "
"Wow, look at you .... This is a real improvement. I'll bet
you feel good about that ... " "I like [or I'm so proud of]
the way you ... "

Part V: Making Appreciation a Habit

Very Rewarding

It is a great mistake for men to give up paying compliments, for when they give up saying what is charming, they give up thinking what is charming.
—*Oscar Wilde*

❦ To Think About: A family member's special moment of personal achievement deserves our appreciation. We honor work well done, perseverance that has paid off. Our peer's recognition, or an audience's applause—each are validations of a family member's accomplishments. The pride and appreciation expressed at such important times, particularly by family, make a profound impact.

What "rewards" are valued most by the various members in your family? Does someone prefer generous words of praise? Extra time together? The display of a piece of work or a trophy? Cash gifts? Peer recognition? The kind of reward one person deeply values may not mean as much to the next person. The rewards people find the most deeply satisfying vary a great deal.

This should influence our approaches to appreciation. One child may work hard to receive good grades for a cash reward. To another, the most desirable payoff might be a teacher's recognition or being featured in the school newspaper. Some work hardest for their own approval. What others think or say at school is of only secondary importance. (It's still worthy of appreciation, however.)

❧ To Do: Over dinner or as you drive somewhere, initiate a family conversation about rewards and the kind of acknowledgment each family member prefers. (It doesn't have to be just one.) Start the conversation by asking, "Of all the rewards you've ever received for an accomplishment, which one stands out in your mind as the most satisfying?"

Around a home or child's bedroom, the most common rewards for achievement—ribbons, trophies, certificates—are easily displayed. As you identify other kinds of rewards begin to look for ways to display and appreciate those. For example, photocopy the school papers and reports upon which the teacher has written positive comments and frame them as a collage. Frame a photocopy of a bonus check earned. When a boss praises your child, write out the words of praise and post them for all to see. Frame that newspaper article about your child's science fair success, or about the community event Dad or Mom worked so hard on. (Highlight the person's name if it appeared in the text.)

Start a scrapbook in which to keep papers and photos, and assign a page upon which you list smaller accomplishments.

Don't forget what you've learned here about each other. Keep it in mind as you plan birthdays and other celebrations for that person in the months and years ahead.

Appreciating Younger Children

The smartest advice on raising children is to enjoy them while they are still on your side.

—Unknown

🌰 **To Think About:** On Day 3 of this project, we thought about how self-esteem is the foundation for healthy living and relationships. We defined self-esteem as *"the sense of being lovable and capable."* We looked at how appreciation is an especially powerful tool for convincing a child that he or she is valuable, loved and capable of reaching the full potential of his or her gifts and abilities. As we said earlier, parental responses are the "mirror" that crafts much of what a child comes to believe about him- or herself and who he or she is.

Your child is young only once. Ask parents of older children and they will tell you those early years pass ever so quickly. You will feel a sense of the urgency if you consider the short time with your child to be like working with wet cement; it remains receptive to your input for only a fleeting handful of years.

➤ **To Do:** Read each of the following suggestions, and place a check mark in front of the ones you can readily use. Then jot on your weekly calendar some specific times and application points.

☐ Appreciate the small accomplishments. The big ones will take care of themselves. Don't wait for your child to complete a major task before you show your encouragement and support.

☐ Play often with your child—two or five or ten minutes of time invested frequently builds the relationship. If your child feels your presence often, he or she won't be so reluctant to let you go when you say you must.

☐ It is estimated that the average child asks 500,000 questions by the age of fifteen. Try hard not to waste a single one of these "teachable moments."

☐ Instead of nagging, yelling, and getting frustrated at having to remind your child to do a chore, write it down on a yellow sticky-note: "Hi, Mark. I know you are busy with school work and soccer practice, but don't forget to feed Penny—Love ya, Mom." For younger children, draw simple pictures of the task—a bed, a dog with a bowl, a tooth brush—with a little check-off box.

☐ State the positive behavior you want instead of the negative outcome you detest. "I want you to pick up your toys now" is much better than "Stop making such a mess."

☐ Does your child hear you use the words "please" and "thank you"? Modeling is always a more powerful way to teach than nagging.

☐ Kids are born with a natural motivation to learn, grow, and contribute. Be careful how many times you say, "You're too little to help. You don't know what to do." Or . . . "You'll break [drop, hurt, wreck] it. When you get a little older you can do it. Go watch a video, or go play!" Too many doses of discouragement can easily yield an I-can't-ever-do-it-so-why-try attitude and a lack of self-confidence. A few years later, when you want your child's help, you'll have a difficult time undoing all the negative feedback.

☐ On a poster in your child's room keep a running list of the skills he or she has learned. Try to add to it several times a week. As you list the newest skill, verbally express your appreciation for the way you see your child using other skills to help you and the family.

Part V: Making Appreciation a Habit
Appreciating Older Children

The memory is a wonderful treasure chest for those
who know how to pack it.

—Unknown

🐦 **To Think About:** From the start, ever since
we can remember, each of us have sought the
praise of our parents and others we respect.
Whether the parent/child relationship during the

younger years was strong or unhealthy, young people still
want an approval bank-account into which generous
deposits are currently being made. It is quite clear to them
whether a parent's approval is rooted in unconditional
love or is performance based. When they fail the parent or
themselves, they need to be able to draw upon the
reserves in their appreciation account.

Consider these words of Adele Faber: "When a teen
pushes parents away in the journey toward independence,
parents often respond by distancing themselves. Think of
the parent/teen relationship as two people at opposite
ends of the same rope, each tugging. If you both keep tugging while also negotiating, you get closer to the middle.
But if you let go of the rope, your child falls down completely, and may be in trouble."

🐦 **To Do:** As you did on Day 27, read each of the following suggestions and place a check mark in front of each
one you can readily use. Jot on your weekly calendar the
specific times and application points.

 What seems trivial to parents is often earthshaking
to a teen. So keep your ears open to show that you
genuinely value what your young person shares with

you. Every day, ask about school, friends, and interests. Use open-ended questions, like: "What was the best [craziest, happiest, hardest] thing that happened in your day, today?" You must care enough to listen to your child's stories and struggles without passing judgment.

☐ The giving of generous nurturance to a teen is not the same as being too soft or coddling. Love and limits must both be at play in the parent/teen relationship.

☐ Just because your young person seems more interested in being with friends than with you, don't be misled. Every teen needs and wants his or her parents to be his or her greatest fans and cheerleaders. Showing up at games and other events, providing transportation when your son or daughter and friends need a ride, being there to celebrate your teen's successes all are powerful ways to express acceptance and appreciation.

☐ Major on the majors. Say "yes" to your child as much as possible. Pick your battles carefully.

☐ Keep the rules to a minimum, but enforce consistently those you establish.

☐ Regularly "date" your daughter. Set weekly or bi-monthly breakfast appointments with your son. Such commitments written on your calendar, like every other important meeting, demonstrate your child's priority in your life and guarantee that you're in touch.

Part V: Making Appreciation a Habit

Through Grateful Eyes

There is likely to be a direct connection between a person's thankfulness to God and his expressions of appreciation to fellow human beings.
—*From* Building Stronger Families

❦ **To Think About:** Parenting is not a sprint, it's a marathon. At the finish line each thought- ful parent hopes to find children who have become humane, compassionate, strong, and confident individuals. Because every family and life expe- rience is marked by events—even tragedies—far beyond our control, the ability to be grateful for each day's delights, gifts, and blessings is a critical appreciation skill. Grateful "eyes" and a grateful heart are cultivated princi- pally through modeling. Parents set the pace.

➤ **To Do:** Keeping a family "Gratefulness Journal" is a powerful and practical place to start. Find an attractive blank book or a simple wire-bound notebook that you can keep at the kitchen table. At mealtimes, or whenever two or more of the family are gathered, take it in hand and record your gratefulness for the blessings you have experienced and noticed that day. Record as well the insights that allow you to be grateful for life's hard and tough moments, such as being held accountable for mis- takes and breaking the rules.

This week-by-week record of your gratitudes is a won- derful way to keep the appreciation flowing and is a pow- erful reminder to review on Thanksgiving Day and at other special times throughout the year. This journal can keep alive much of what your family has been learning and practicing throughout this project.

Another helpful tool is a supply of note cards kept next to the table (or tucked into the journal) on which you jot words of appreciation to anyone who has done something helpful, or inspired you in any way. Even your youngest child can put grateful thoughts into words that you can write on notes and into the journal.

Use those moments when you are making a journal entry as a time of spiritual refreshment, gratitude, prayer, and thankfulness. Pay particular attention to expressing gratitude for each family member—all that aggravates you and all that makes you laugh!

Time-Out!

We Can Appreciate Clearly Now

Being a parent is a tug-of-war between who we think
we should be and who we actually are; between what
we want to do and what we are actually able to do.
—*Stephanie Marston*

DAY 30

For thirty days now, your family has been discovering the value of expressing appreciation. You are recognizing the skills that make appreciation a well-honed and fruitful family habit. As this special project comes to a close, how are you doing? What have you learned together? Is expressed appreciation making a fresh difference in your family? Does anyone feel left out of the fun?

The answers may be found in what each family member would say if he or she spoke completely from the heart with love and compassion. So, on this thirtieth day, take time for some "heart-talk." Here's how:

"Heart-talk" happens when you can have an unhurried "family meeting." Ideally, family appreciation will be the sole item on your agenda. Provide some coloring books or another quiet activity to keep the hands of young children busy while you talk. Snacks can also help "heart-talk" flow more naturally.

Before you begin, search around the house for a heart-shaped object to serve as your "talking heart." (It could be a piece of jewelry, a cookie cutter, a small box, or a heart cutout from construction paper.)

Take turns holding the "talking heart" and speak about what this appreciation project has meant to you personally. Follow these simple rules:

- Only the person holding the heart can speak. Everyone else listens with full attention and support. Keep your turns to two or three minutes in length. Each person can take several turns.
- Pass (don't toss) the "talking heart" gently to the person on your left.
- If a person doesn't wish to share, the heart is simply passed to the next person.
- Talk about what you feel or think and not about what someone else has said.
- Above all, create a safe, nonjudgmental atmosphere so everyone feels they can speak freely.

The topics for this "heart-talk" session could be:

- How our family feels as a result of expressing appreciation
- What I have learned about appreciation
- How various expressions of appreciation make me feel
- How I plan to keep going in this area
- (For the person who didn't participate much) What I think about this kind of family project

At the close of this "heart-talk" meeting, jot on Appreciation Bookmark No. 4, at the back of this section, the most important thoughts expressed by family members. Then note the practical ideas and steps your family will use to keep strengthening your relationships by expressing appreciation, including use of a personal and/or family Gratefulness Journal.

Appreciation Bookmark No. 1

I pledge my participation in this family project. I will listen, think hard, do the assignments, and try my best. Over the next 25 days we will improve on expressing appreciation in this family!

30 DAYS TO A SMART FAMILY

Signed _____

Signed _____

Signed _____

Signed _____

Signed _____

Part II: Clearing Hurdles Topics:

- **A Weak Foundation** *(day)*
  Overcoming poor parenting models

- **Gifts Out of Control** *(day)*
  The dark side of personal strengths

- **Crushing Criticism** *(day)*
  The unholy power of negative feedback

- **Moon Shots** *(day)*
  Managing unrealistic expectations

Appreciation Bookmark No. 2

30 DAYS TO A SMART FAMILY

Part III: What to Appreciate

- **Doin' What Comes Naturally**
  Appreciating natural gifts and abilities
  _____ *(day)*

- **Character Strengths**
  Physical and emotional contributions
  _____ *(day)*

- **Home Work**
  Appreciating chores and house-hold tasks
  _____ *(day)*

- **Great Choices**
  Appreciating wise decisions
  _____ *(day)*

Appreciation Bookmark No. 3

Part IV: How to Appreciate Skills

- **Word Power**
  Spoken appreciation
  _____ *(day)*

- **26 Mighty Soldiers**
  Written appreciation
  _____ *(day)*

- **You've Got the Touch**
  Appreciative hugs and pats
  _____ *(day)*

- **Giving an Eyeful**
  Appreciative looks and body language
  _____ *(day)*

- **I Caught You!**
  Noticing right actions to appreciate
  _____ *(day)*

- **The Feelings Detective**
  Appreciating by understanding feelings
  _____ *(day)*

Appreciation Bookmark No. 4

The best thoughts shared during our "Heart-Talk" family meeting were:

_____

_____

_____

_____

30 DAYS TO A SMART FAMILY

Ideas and steps to keep our appreciation flowing:

_____

_____

_____

_____

Appreciation
Bookmark No. 4

30 DAYS SMART FAMILY

Family project notes:

Appreciation
Bookmark No. 3

30 DAYS SMART FAMILY

Family project notes:

Appreciation
Bookmark No. 2

30 DAYS SMART FAMILY

Family project notes:

Appreciation
Bookmark No. 1

30 DAYS SMART FAMILY

Family project notes:

Here's More Help to Apply
30 Days to a Smart Family
Three additional

30-DAY GUIDEBOOKS
on key family growth issues

*E*ach 30-Day Guidebook in this expanding series will help any concerned family create a family project to solve a problem or begin to grow in a particular area of family life. Every Guidebook follows the pattern of Part III of this book. Each is 48-64 pages of practical suggestions and a simple 30-day plan for your family to customize.

• *Sharing the Load*
How to Improve Teamwork in Your Family
64 pages, $4.99

• *Building Bridges*
Improving a Troubled Family Relationship
48 pages, $4.99

• *Money$ense*
Getting Control of Your Family Finances
64 pages, $4.99

Smart Families Start Here™...

FAMILY UNIVERSITY,

a "university without walls," is helping fathers, mothers, and children, as well as single, step- and grandparents, learn the time-

less secrets for enjoying close and satisfying family relationships. The Family University curriculum brings to enrolled families the finest in family-skills publications, audio and video programs, resources via the World Wide Web, educational seminars, and a library of books and mixed-media resources.

Smart Families/Smart Business™ is a Family University

global business initiative led by FORTUNE 500 companies committed to helping employee families "blend" their work and family priorities. For information on how to enroll your employee or constituent families and how to join the Global Campus Network, contact the Office of the Director of Global Campus Development.

✍ *Smart families may individually enroll* in the annual curriculum by contacting Family University at the toll-free number or on the World Wide Web.

Internet: www.familyuniversity.com
Family University Resources: 1-800-255-3237

National Offices: FAMILY UNIVERSITY, LLC, P.O. Box 500050, San Diego, CA 92150-0050
Voice: 619-487-7099 • Fax: 619-487-7356

Enrollment in the annual curriculum brings 16 family-building tools to your kitchen table.